YOU'RE A DAD NOW

FIRST-TIME PREGNANCY GUIDE FOR NEW DADS

I0167899

A Month-by-Month Modern Survival Guide with
Expert Tips, Real Talk, and Step-by-Step Advice for
Pregnancy, Birth, and Your New Baby

**Cameron Friel with
Dr. Rhowela A. Friel, PharmD**

DISCLAIMER

This book is here to share ideas, stories, and tips from one dad to another. My co-author fact-checked everything, but the voice here is mine. It's not a replacement for real medical advice. If you've got health questions—about you, your partner, or your baby—always talk to a licensed healthcare provider before starting, changing, or stopping any treatment or medication.

I've done my best to keep the info accurate and useful, but things change, and I can't promise it's perfect for every situation. I'm not responsible for any injury, loss, or "well, that didn't work" moments that might happen from using this book.

Any brands, products, or medications mentioned are just examples—not endorsements. All trademarks belong to their rightful owners.

By reading this, you agree I'm not liable for any direct or indirect damages that may come from using it. This reflects my knowledge and experience at the time I wrote it, and—like parenting itself—it may evolve as time goes on.

Juniper Dylan Press
Murrieta, California
www.juniperdylanpress.com

DEDICATION

To my wife, who lived every page with me, caught my typos
(and my diaper disasters), and made sure I got the facts straight
while keeping it real. Thanks for helping me write this the
way we lived it—side by side.

And to you, the new dad holding this book, probably wondering what the
hell you just signed up for: you don't need to know everything.
You just need to show up—and keep showing up.

WELCOME!

Alright, man—first things first: you're not behind. You're exactly where you're supposed to be.

Maybe your partner handed you this book. Maybe you grabbed it yourself because things just got very real. Either way, you opened it, and that counts. You showed up. And that's the whole game.

If your partner wants her own playbook, send her to rhowelaafriel.com. My wife built it for first-time moms who want straight answers without the fluff. She's a pharmacist who made sure this book is more than just jokes and good vibes.

But this book? This is your side of the story—what it really means to be a first-time dad: showing up, staying grounded, and backing your growing team. Grab a pen, dog-ear some pages, and keep this thing close. You'll probably end up reading it in a hospital chair, at the kitchen counter during a midnight feeding, or while raiding the pantry at 3 a.m.

That's exactly how it's supposed to be.

Let's get to it.

TABLE OF CONTENTS

INTRODUCTION
WELCOME TO FIRST-TIME
DAD MODE

Hey man,

If you're reading this, you probably just found out you're gonna be a dad… or maybe you're a few months in, scrolling articles and forums at 2 a.m., thinking, Wait—do I actually know what I'm doing?

Good. You're in the right place.

Not because I've got it all figured out—but because I absolutely didn't. I've been where you are—excited, nervous, confused, and just one internet search away from, Is it normal to tear up during a diaper commercial?

My wife wrote a pregnancy book for first-time moms—calm, clear, and super helpful. I read it and thought, Cool… but where's the one for dads?

Not the stiff medical manual. Not the eye-roll, just be supportive one-liner. A real guide—from a guy who's actually been there.

So we made one.

This is my voice—dad to dad, rookie to rookie. My wife's a pharmacist, and she fact-checked every page. I ran everything through one test: Would I actually say this to a buddy at 2 a.m. mid-diaper blowout?

If not, it didn't make the cut.

What You'll Learn

This book walks you month by month through pregnancy and baby prep. From We're pregnant to We're in the hospital to Holy crap, there's a baby in our house.

It's designed to give you real tools, clear advice, and the dad tips you didn't know you needed.

Inside, you'll find:

- What's happening to her body, and how you can actually be useful instead of just standing there.
- What's going on in your brain, because yeah—your identity's shifting too.
- What to say, do, bring, and know so you don't freeze like a deer in headlights.
- How to show up at appointments, during labor, and in those weird in-between moments.
- What actually changes after the baby arrives: mentally, emotionally, and logistically.

Who This Book Is For

- You just found out and you're freaking out
- You've been trying for years and now it's finally happening
- You're excited but also anxious
- You're not sure you're ready (but you want to be)
- You're parenting from a distance
- You want to support your partner but don't know how
- You didn't have a great role model and want to do better

If any of that hits? This book's for you.

Why This Book Is Different

There's no shortage of parenting books. But most either talk at dads—or worse, talk about us.

This one talks to you—like a guy who's been there, still figuring it out. Not a superhero. Just a present, emotionally available partner who shows up.

It's built from real first-time dad experience and backed by pharmacist-reviewed, medically sound info—so you're not winging it with a half-charged phone and no clue.

What You'll Get from This Book

For the skimmers and the sleep-deprived, this book's broken into quick, useful parts you'll read along the way:

- 💡 **Dad Tip:** clear, usable takeaways that actually help

- 🐣 **Sanity Checks:** quick mental resets to help you breathe and recalibrate

- ☑ **Checklists:** what to pack, prep, and say—without overthinking it

- 🗣 **Partner Scripts:** ready-to-use lines for when you've got no clue what to say

- 🎮 **Mini-Guides & Bonuses:** deeper dives on stuff like birth plans and baby gear

- 💬 **Reflection Prompts:** fast gut-checks to keep you grounded

- 🎙 **Real Talk:** personal stories from my own first-time dad experience

Grab Your Free Book Bonuses

You'll find checklists, dad tips, partner scripts, and action steps throughout this book—from pregnancy to postpartum. But you don't have to flip back and forth every time you need something.

Scan the QR code or visit [subscribepage.io/juniperdylan-bonuses] to grab your free printable bonus bundle:

- Early Dad Game Plan
- Dad Leave Cheat Sheet
- Birth Plan Snapshot
- Hospital Bag Checklist for Dads
- Month-by-Month Dad Survival Guide

You'll get these as PDFs straight to your inbox—no fluff, just real tools to keep you ahead of the chaos.

BEFORE WE GET INTO IT...

Being a dad doesn't start in the delivery room.

It starts now. By showing up, asking questions, and giving a damn. That's why this book exists—to help you feel ready when it matters most.

PART 1

BEFORE THE BUMP–WHAT TO KNOW RIGHT AWAY

*"The nature of impending fatherhood is that you are
doing something you're unqualified to do, and then you become
qualified while doing it."*
—John Green

This is where it actually starts.

Not the hospital. Not the baby kicks. Not even that first ultrasound.

For me, it started with a phone call—from my girlfriend, after the fertility clinic told her we were pregnant. There was no dramatic music, no emotional monologue. Just a quiet moment where everything shifted.

That's when it hit me: I'm in this now. And I have no idea what I'm doing.

But that's the job. You don't start qualified—you get there by showing up, one step at a time. This part isn't about knowing everything. It's about learning to pay attention, support without fixing, and build the mindset of a guy who's ready to grow into the role.

This section is your warm-up lap. A reset. A way to get your head in the game before everything speeds up. Let's get you from "uhh, what do I do?" to "okay, I've got this."

No pressure to be perfect. But you're here—and that already counts.

1.1: WE'RE PREGNANT—NOW WHAT?

I wasn't supposed to get that call.

We'd just gotten serious. Serious like, "Do you want kids someday?" and "Which one of our awful couches has to go?" We knew it might be tough. She had polycystic ovary syndrome (PCOS), and my swimmers weren't exactly gunning for gold.

Then boom—fertility clinic. One try. Odds weren't in our favor. Most couples have maybe a one-in-four shot each month. With PCOS in the mix, it usually takes longer. But somehow… it happened.

I expected more tries. More time to process. More late-night talks and maybe one last trip.

But then the call came.

"We're pregnant."

And I froze.

My mouth said, "Wait… really?"

My brain went straight to spreadsheet panic mode—alarms blaring, sirens wailing.

My heart? Somewhere between thrilled and completely losing it.

Here's what no one tells you: finding out you're gonna be a dad feels like someone handed you a live grenade, smiled, and whispered, "Don't drop it."

I felt happy. I also felt terrified, unqualified, and a little bit like I was watching someone else's life unfold in front of me.

No one tells you how weirdly lonely that moment can be. People congratulate you—sure. But no one checks if you're quietly spiraling. You're supposed to be chill. Supportive. Stoic. Confident.

But what if you're not?

Maybe it wasn't expected. Or maybe it took years of trying to get here. Either way—it's okay if your emotions are messy. You can feel grateful and overwhelmed. Hopeful and off-balance. You're allowed to hold more than one truth at once.

What if you're sitting there wondering how the hell you're gonna afford diapers—or whether you're even cut out for this?

That's normal, man.

You don't have to nail it on day one.

You just have to show up.

Forget parenting philosophies and color-coded to-do lists. Just show up. That's it.

Early Dad Moves That Matter
Here's how to show up early—even if you don't feel ready yet:

- Ask how she's doing—not like you're checking a box. Actually ask.
- Offer to schedule the first doctor's appointment.
- Download a pregnancy app and laugh at whatever fruit your baby is this week.
- Say "We've got this"—even if you don't totally believe it yet.

💡 Dad Tip
Confidence isn't knowing what you're doing. It's showing up anyway. Say the words. Be there. That's how this starts.

Ignore These (For Now)
You're gonna feel pressure—from your own head, from social media, from dumb comments at work. Here's what to tune out while you find your footing:

- That voice whispering, "You're not ready."
- Perfect social media baby reveals—matching onesies, smoke cannons, the whole production.

- Pressure to be stoic, chill, or act like you're fine. You're allowed to feel all of it.

💬 **Reflection Prompt:**
Gut-check time: What's the realest thing you're feeling right now? And what's one move you can make this week—even if you're not totally ready—to show up anyway?

🧠 **Dad Sanity Check:**
- Am I pretending I'm fine—or actually giving myself space to deal with this?
- Who's one person I can talk to (friend, brother, therapist) without feeling like I'm blowing it?
- What's one fear I haven't said out loud yet—but probably should?

1.2: SURVIVAL TIP #1—SUPPORT WITHOUT FIXING EVERYTHING

Still trying to wrap your head around "we're pregnant"? I was right there with you. I was catching my breath when my wife hit me with something I never saw coming.

She looked at me, dead serious, and said, "I feel ugly. Like I'm disappearing. Like this body isn't mine anymore."

I froze. Gut reaction? Fix it. So I launched into what I thought was a supportive speech: "You're beautiful. You're doing everything right. The doctor said it's all normal…"

I meant every word. None of it landed.

She didn't need reassurance. She needed to not feel alone.

She needed someone to sit in the storm with her—not try to blow the clouds away. Someone to say, "Yeah, that sucks," and just stay.

That's when it hit me:

Support isn't fixing. It's witnessing.

When your partner's upset, your reflex might be to help. Same here. But sometimes helping turns into solving problems she never asked you to fix. And that can leave her feeling unheard.

Here's one move that changed the game for me:

"Do you want comfort or solutions?"

Simple. Respectful. And it keeps you from accidentally mansplaining her feelings back to her.

Pregnancy is a wild ride: hormones, fatigue, mood swings, fear, joy, rage. It's all part of it. Your job isn't to dodge it or fix it. It's to be steady through it.

Sometimes that means being quiet.

Sometimes it means saying, "That sucks."

Sometimes it means doing the dishes—without acting like you just ended world hunger.

It doesn't have to be complicated.

It just has to be real.

💡 Dad Tip: Be Her Calm, Not Her Consultant
Ask if she wants comfort or solutions. Then zip it and follow her lead. Silence can be powerful, and showing up is support.

☑ Quick Wins Checklist
Not sure where to start? Here are the little things that actually help—and the stuff that'll backfire fast.

Stuff That Helps:

- Say, "That sounds rough. I'm here." Then mean it.
- Don't rush to fix—just stay close.

- Handle one or two of her usual daily things—without narrating it.
- Bring snacks, water, or a blanket—a quiet ninja-care move.
- Show up with presence, not a five-point plan.

Stuff That Definitely Doesn't:

- "Relax."
- "You're overthinking it."
- "It's not that bad."
- Anything starting with "You should…" (just... don't)

👤 **Script Swap: From Fixing to Showing Up**

When you're tempted to fix it, swap the script instead. Here's how to trade "oops" lines for ones that actually land.

Instead of...	Try Saying...
"Relax."	"That sounds rough. I'm here."
"You're overthinking it."	"You've got a lot on your mind—I get it."
"It's not that bad."	"That sucks. Want to talk about it or just vent?"
"You should…"	"Want me to just listen or help figure it out?"

💭 **Reflection Prompt**

What's one moment recently when just listening might've helped more than diving in with advice?

🧠 **Dad Sanity Check**

- When was the last time I tried to fix something she didn't ask me to?
- Can I sit with discomfort—or do I rush to fill silence with solutions?
- What's one way I can show support this week without needing credit?

This skill? You'll need it even more during postpartum—when emotions run hotter and sleep runs low.

1.3: SURVIVAL TIP #2—HOW TO SEARCH SMART (AND STAY SANE)

Two nights after we found out we were pregnant, I was on the couch, lit by the glow of my phone, deep in a 2:47 a.m. Reddit spiral about missed miscarriages and "what that cramping really means."

Did I walk away feeling informed? Nope. Just overwhelmed. I felt like I was starring in a psychological thriller called "Pregnancy Panic: Dad Edition."

I was just trying to get ahead of things, to feel ready. But instead, I ended up scrolling through horror stories, miracle crystals, and one guy's 17-paragraph theory involving moon phases. I wanted clarity. I got chaos.

My wife eventually woke up, clocked the wild look in my eyes, and gently took the phone out of my hands like it was a weapon—because it was.

That's when it hit me: searching online can be helpful. But it can also absolutely wreck your mental state.

You're gonna look stuff up. Obviously. That's just what we do now. And sometimes, it is helpful: knowing what to ask at appointments, checking safe meds, figuring out what food she suddenly can't eat anymore. Fine.

But there's a line where info-seeking turns into doom-scrolling.

Ten open tabs. Zero peace of mind. Sound familiar?

That's not research—that's anxiety in a costume.

Here's what I learned the hard way:

If you don't know what a reliable source looks like, every symptom becomes a worst-case scenario. Don't do that to yourself, man.

💡 **Dad Tip: Look It Up—But Set Limits**
Look it up but stick to trusted sources. If it's 3 a.m. and you feel worse, not better, close the tab and go to bed.

Helpful vs. Harmful Searches

Not all searches are created equal. Here's a quick cheat sheet to help you spot what's actually useful—and what's just panic fuel.

Helpful	Harmful
"First trimester symptoms checklist"	"Can cramps mean miscarriage?"
"What to ask at first OB visit"	"Does feeling unready mean I'll be a bad dad?"
"Safe OTC meds during pregnancy"	"Missed miscarriage stories Reddit"
"When should I go to appointments?"	"How do people survive twins with no sleep?"

Trusted Resources (For Real):

When in doubt, skip the forums and stick to the pros. These are the sites and apps you can trust without spiraling.

- **Mayo Clinic**—clear, solid, no fluff
- **ACOG**—the American College of Obstetricians & Gynecologists—expert-backed, no nonsense
- **HealthyChildren.org**—from the AAP, legit pediatric info
- **DaddyUp App**—solid info, dad-friendly tone

Want more solid sources? Flip to the **"Further Reading and Resources"** section at the back.

☑ **Quick Wins Checklist**

Stuff That's Actually Worth Looking Up:

- What to ask at your first OB visit
- Early pregnancy symptoms (fatigue, nausea, cravings)
- Safe snacks and over-the-counter meds

- What appointments you should show up for—hint: pretty much all of them, if possible

Stuff You Should Not Look Up at 2 a.m.:

- "Spotting week 6 miscarriage or implantation"
- "No heartbeat at first scan"
- "PCOS pregnancy horror stories"
- Anything that starts with "Is it normal if…"

💬 **Reflection Prompt**

What's one question you've been too nervous—or too overwhelmed—to ask your partner or her doctor?

1.4: PARTNER PRIORITIES—FIRST APPOINTMENTS, EARLY SYMPTOMS, AND EMOTIONAL SWINGS

I'll admit it—I blew the first OB appointment.

I showed up thinking my job was to be moral support—sit quietly, nod, maybe throw in a concerned eyebrow. Then on the way home, she asked me to remind her what the doctor said about early symptoms.

And I had nothing. Total blank. I remembered the room had chairs. That's it.

She didn't get mad, but I could feel it. A quiet letdown. She needed me tuned in—not just there, physically. That's when I realized—this isn't just her appointment. It's ours.

I want you to be more prepared than I was. Here's what I wish I'd done differently—and what actually helps in those early weeks.

The Early Weeks Are Weird. And Heavy.

Her body's running a full system update in the background. Hormones are off the charts. She might cry during an insurance commercial, fall asleep mid-conversation, or crave frozen pickles at 1 a.m. None of this is exaggeration.

Some days she'll want cuddles and reassurance. Other days—silence, snacks, and absolutely zero unsolicited opinions. That's not about you—it's hormones doing donuts in her brain and body.

Your role? Show up. Be calm. Be her steady point in all this chaos.

First Appointments: What You Can Actually Do
Don't just sit there like a spare tire. These are the simple moves that make you useful in the room—and still involved if you can't be there in person.

- If you're allowed in, go. Seriously. Being there says more than anything you could say.
- Bring a short list of questions. Ask her what she's wondering too.
- Jot down a few key notes. It'll help her remember later and make you look like a pro.
- Ask the OB what to expect in the coming weeks—it shows you're paying attention.

If you can't attend in person:

- Be part of the prep. Help her write down questions ahead of time.
- Follow up afterward. Showing interest still counts.

Five Questions That Make You Look Like a Pro (Even Quietly)
You don't need a medical degree. Just these five questions will make the OB (and your partner) see that you're dialed in.

1. What's the due date, based on today?
2. Are there early symptoms—or red flags—we should look out for?
3. What tests or scans are coming soon?
4. What foods or meds should we avoid?
5. When's our next appointment, and what should we be ready for?

Dad Deep Dive: What She Can't Eat (And Why You Should Know)

Your job isn't to be the food police—but you do need to know what's off-limits. Pregnancy flips the menu. Her immune system's running with less defense, and some foods that were harmless before can now carry real risks.

Here's your don't be that guy cheat sheet:

Avoid These	Why It's Out
Unpasteurized soft cheeses (brie, feta, blue cheese)	Listeria risk—can cause miscarriage or preterm birth
Cold deli meats & hot dogs (unless heated until steaming)	Listeria again—reheat like you mean it
Undercooked eggs (runny yolks, homemade mayo)	Salmonella is a no-go
Raw seafood (sushi, oysters)	Parasites and bacteria—just nope
High-mercury fish (shark, swordfish, king mackerel)	Can mess with baby's brain development
Alcohol	No safe amount found—support her by skipping it or keeping it subtle

What's Still Safe (in moderation):
- Coffee (up to 200mg/day—about one small cup)
- Fully cooked fish (salmon, shrimp, tilapia)
- Pasteurized dairy (yogurt, milk, hard cheeses)
- Fully cooked eggs

♀ Dad Tip

About to surprise her with food? Double-check it first. Don't guess. Use Mayo Clinic, ACOG, or HealthyChildren.org. Search smart, not scared.

🧠 Dad Sanity Check
- Have I offered her anything sketchy this week—without realizing it?
- What's one meal I can prep or pick up that says "I've got you"?

Mood Swings Are Real. So Is the Pressure.

This is not the time to expect consistency. Some days she'll want to vent, cry, snack, nap, and rage—all before lunch. Other days she might act like everything's fine but still be carrying ten layers of physical and emotional stress under the surface. She's not pushing you away. She's just running on fumes.

Don't try to fix it. Just stay close. Let her ride the wave, knowing you're there when she needs a hand.

Symptom Cheat Sheet (a.k.a Why She's Wiped Out)

Here's your translator for the first trimester. When she says she's exhausted or snaps at you over snacks, this is what's really going on—and how you can actually help.

Symptom	What It Means or How to Help
Fatigue	This isn't "sleepy." It's full battery drain. Support naps guilt-free.
Nausea	Not just mornings. Keep ginger ale and crackers on standby.
Mood Swings	Hormones are doing parkour. Don't take it personally.
Tender Breasts	Yes, they hurt. Even hugs can suck. Ask first.
Frequent Peeing	Just know where the bathrooms are. That's the move.
Cramping or Spotting	Can be normal—but help her bring it up to the OB if anything feels off.

⚠ **REMINDER:** You're not a doctor. If something feels off, call the real one. That's not overreacting—it's being responsible.

☑ Quick Wins Checklist
Here's how to show up where it counts—both in the exam room and back at home. Small moves, big impact.

At the Appointment:

- Ask her, "Want me to bring anything up for you?"
- Write down a couple of takeaways—next steps, tests, dates.
- Confirm next steps before you leave.
- Say "thank you" to her afterward. This moment is huge.

At Home:

- Stock the go-to snacks.
- Offer foot rubs, back rubs—or quiet time, if that's what she needs.
- Take on little errands or chores without being asked.
- Be cool with the emotional curveballs. This phase is wild.

🗨 **Reflection Prompt**

What's one small thing you can take off her plate this week—and one real question you want to ask at the next appointment?

1.5: THE EARLY DAD GEAR CHECKLIST— WHAT YOU ACTUALLY NEED

When we found out we were pregnant, I didn't buy anything. Not a book. Not a bib. Not even one of those "funny" dad mugs.

It's not that I didn't care. I just didn't know where to start. She was already ten steps ahead, tracking symptoms in an app while I was still deciding if we were telling people or playing it cool. I assumed I'd be more useful later—once stuff needed building or sanitizing. Looking back, I wish someone had told me:

You don't need gear to start being a dad—you just need to start acting like one.

Gear Won't Make You Ready. Habits Will

Early pregnancy isn't about buying things. It's about how you show up when there's nothing flashy to do.

Your partner is already carrying the weight—literally and emotionally. What helps her most right now? Your consistency. Your effort. Your attention to the stuff she shouldn't have to manage alone.

That means setting up a few systems. Getting yourself organized. Staying looped in. It's not glamorous, but it's the good stuff.

This isn't a shopping list. Think of it as your starter game plan.

Not Ready for Gear? Start Here Instead
Forget the shopping cart—build these habits first:

- Check in daily—and ask how she's really doing.
- Own your calendar. Plug in all her key dates.
- Be snack-aware—master that skill early.

These habits show up louder than anything you can buy.

Starter Kit Box: 7 Things Every Dad Should Have by Month 2
Think of this as your first dad loadout. Not gear for the baby—gear for you to actually show up and stay organized by Month 2.

1. **Shared calendar access:** Put OB appointments, important dates, and "do not book a meeting" days in your calendar too.
2. **A pregnancy app:** DaddyUp has a dad voice. The Bump or What to Expect are solid too. Know what size your baby is today—fruit or otherwise.
3. **Shared notes file:** Track doctor questions, name ideas, weird cravings. If it's not written down, it's gone.
4. **Comfort item for her:** Heating pad, sea bands, fuzzy socks—something that says, "I see you, and I've got you."
5. **Emergency snacks:** For both of you—trust me on this one.
6. **One go-to support contact:** A buddy or sibling you can call when you're quietly freaking out.
7. **A simple weekly ritual:** A walk, a check-in, a "how are we really doing?" moment. Small, regular, and hers too.

💡 Dad Tip: Show Up Early—Even If You're Not Buying Stuff Yet

Forget the fancy gadgets—build the habits that make her life easier and show her you're in it from day one.

☑ Quick Wins Checklist

Skip the overthinking. These are the early moves that actually help—and the stuff you can ignore for now.

Early moves that actually help:

- Ask her what makes her feel more comfortable right now
- Put all doctor appointments in your calendar (with reminders)
- Start and maintain a shared Notes app or doc
- Keep a snack drawer stocked—salty, bland, whatever works

Stuff to skip (for now):

- Designer diaper bags
- Overpriced baby monitors she won't use for 6 months
- Debating baby names in week 5
- Comparing yourself to social media dads with color-coordinated nurseries

💬 Reflection Prompt

What's one small system or habit you can set up this week to make things smoother for both of you?

🎯 Mini Dad Log

No pressure. Just a few honest thoughts to mark where your head's at right now.

Dad Check-In Prompts:

- What's one thing I did this week to show up?
- What's a question I want to ask her but haven't yet?
- What's my biggest fear right now?
- What am I genuinely excited about?

Write it down, text it to a friend, say it out loud while brushing your teeth. Doesn't matter how—just give yourself the space to check in. That's part of this too.

🧠 Dad Sanity Check

- Have I looked up "Can she eat this?" at least once this week?
- Am I offering meals that actually support her—or just what I'd want?
- What's one craving she's mentioned lately that I can safely deliver?

Before You Start Trimester 1...

You don't need to know everything. No parenting degree required. But you do need to care enough to keep learning—and keep showing up.

These first weeks? They're behind-the-scenes work. She's building a baby from scratch. You're holding up the rest of life. It might not feel like much, but it matters more than either of you might realize yet.

If you've made it this far, you're already doing more than most. Keep going. You're not the sidekick—you're a teammate in this.

Early Dad Game Plan (Also Printable—Check the Intro)

Think of this as your locker-room whiteboard: what to actually do in Weeks 1–12. No matching onesies required. You'll find it again in the printable bonus bundle (QR code's back in the Introduction). Save it, tape it to the fridge, or hand it to your partner to prove you're in "I give a damn" mode.

EARLY DAD GAMEPLAN
Mindset
- Say "We've got this" (even if you're not 100% sure).
- It's okay to feel excited *and* freaked out.
- Show up early. Presence > perfection.

Habits That Win
- **Shared Calendar:** Add appointments, reminders, blocked-off "don't book" days.
- **Shared Notes File:** Track questions, cravings, funny name ideas, and to-dos.
- **Weekly Check-In Ritual:** One real conversation a week: "How are *we* doing?"

Tools That Help
- **Pregnancy App:** Try DaddyUp (dad tone), The Bump, or What to Expect.
- **Support Contact:** A buddy you can text when you're quietly spiraling.
- **Sanity Save:** Keep ginger ale, crackers, and her comfort item on standby.

First Appointment Moves
- Ask if she wants you to bring anything up.
- Jot down 2–3 key takeaways.
- Ask the OB, "What should we expect next?
- Can't attend? Help prep questions and follow up afterward.

Stuff to Skip (For Now)
- Designer gear and nursery themes.
- Reddit spirals at 2 a.m.
- Fixing her feelings instead of witnessing them.
- Acting chill when you're really overwhelmed.

You don't need to know everything yet. You just need to keep showing up.

PART 2

TRIMESTER 1—THE FOG OF FIRSTS (MONTHS 1–3)

"A father carries pictures where his money used to be."
—*Steve Martin*

Trimester 1 hit weird.

We got the call from the clinic. She called me. And boom—we were in it. But not in any way that felt real. No bump. No kicks. Just a few numbers on a chart, and a feeling that I should probably be more excited—but mostly felt confused.

This stretch is like watching the beginning of a movie with the sound off. You know something's happening, but you can't make out the story yet.

She was exhausted. I was trying not to mess anything up. Her body was changing fast. I couldn't see any of it. I wanted to help—but I didn't know what help looked like yet.

This part's about navigating that fog. The symptoms, the emotions, the disconnect—and the small ways you can start showing up even when it feels like you're mostly standing on the sidelines.

Let's break it down—what's happening with her, what might be happening in you—and how to build trust, confidence, and connection in the invisible stage of it all.

2.1: PREGNANCY 101—WHAT'S HAPPENING IN HER BODY... AND YOURS

The day we found out we were pregnant, I looked at my girlfriend and thought, She looks exactly the same.

No baby bump. No magical glow. Just us on the couch, processing the news over leftover noodles.

But something had shifted. She was a little more emotional than usual. Quieter sometimes, snappier other times. She'd go from cuddly to don't touch me in five minutes flat.

At first, I took it personally. I kept wondering, Did I do something wrong? I kept trying to be supportive, but every "Are you okay?" seemed to make things worse. I didn't realize yet that this wasn't about me. It was biology on blast inside her body.

And me? I looked the same too—but I felt different. Jumpier. Quieter. Looking things up I didn't even know how to spell and flinching every time she said ouch.

Welcome to the invisible trimester—everything's changing, but almost nothing shows on the outside.

What's Actually Going Down in Her Body
This first trimester? Pregnancy's installing itself silently in the background—and not gracefully. Her body's working overtime, but unless you've got X-ray vision, you won't see a thing.

Here's a fast-and-real breakdown of what's going on:

- **Hormone surge:** hCG, estrogen, and progesterone spike fast, and they're behind most of the wild stuff: nausea, mood swings, total exhaustion
- **Implantation:** Around the 4th week, the fertilized egg locks in. Some cramping or light spotting? Usually normal—but always worth mentioning to the OB

- **Everything ramps up:** Blood volume increases, her boobs may ache or swell, digestion slows (hello bloat), and her immune system shifts gears to protect the pregnancy

She might feel like absolute garbage—nauseated, bloated, tired, emotionally short-circuited—and still look like nothing's changed.

⚠ **Heads-up**

If she's exhausted, queasy, or snapping at you over snack choices, that's not drama—it's biology.

📖 **Side Plug**

My wife wrote a full pregnancy book for moms while living this. It's way deeper than I can explain here—and I still refer to it when I blank on what trimester we're in. Look it up if you want to really get what's happening.

What Might Be Happening in You

Here's the part no one talks about: this trimester messes with your head too.

You might feel:

- Numb
- Overwhelmed
- Weirdly hyper-aware
- Quietly terrified
- Like you're faking excitement you don't actually feel yet

That's all normal. You're not broken, cold, or selfish if you're not "there" yet emotionally. It's okay if you don't feel bonded yet—connection can come later, and that doesn't make you any less of a dad.

You're trying to make sense of a massive shift that hasn't landed physically in your world yet.

Science backs you up here. Studies suggest expectant dads might see slight drops in testosterone (which may help with bonding) and jumps in cortisol (the stress hormone). Your body's picking up the signal—even if you don't realize it yet.

(See "Trusted Resources & Further Reading" at the end of the book for studies on hormonal shifts in expectant dads, including research from the Mayo Clinic and the American Psychological Association.)

Want to support her? Cool. First, support you. Start by checking in with where your head's really at.

♀ Dad Tip: Start Showing Up Now
Don't wait for the belly to show—she's already in it, and so are you. Ask questions, pay attention, show up.

Partner Wins: Trimester 1 Survival Tips
Here's how to actually help when everything feels invisible and weird. No cape needed—just small, steady moves that make her life a little easier (and show you're already in this).

- Use a pregnancy app (try Mayo Clinic, DaddyUp, or What to Expect) to track what's going on each week
- Ask how she's feeling—and actually listen, without trying to solve anything
- Stock snacks, decaf tea, or comfy socks—whatever helps her feel less miserable
- Remember: just because she looks okay doesn't mean she feels okay
- Give yourself permission to feel weird, disconnected, or out of your depth

TRIMESTER 1 AT A GLANCE

Need the big picture fast? Here's what you're both walking through right now—physically, emotionally, and in your relationship. Scan it, share it, stick it on the fridge if it helps.

Category	What to Expect
Physical (Her)	Nausea, fatigue, bloating, sore boobs, peeing constantly
Emotional (Her)	Mood swings, anxiety, excitement, frustration
Emotional (You)	Shock, guilt, overwhelm, detachment, quiet panic
Relationship Stuff	Fewer date nights, more naps, shorter tempers, and a new need for intentional communication
Partner Wins	Ask how she's feeling, prep appointments, stock snacks, say "I've got you"

💬 Reflection Prompt and 🧠 Dad Sanity Check

- What's something happening in her body right now that you didn't realize?
- What's one small way you can show up for her this week—physically or emotionally?
- Are you feeling like a participant in this pregnancy—or still kind of watching from the sidelines?
- What's one thing you need to take off your own plate so you have more bandwidth for her?

2.2: MORNING SICKNESS & CRAVINGS—WHEN YOU'RE NOT THE ONE BARFING

Week six. I'm reheating leftover brisket in the microwave when I hear gagging behind me. Two seconds later, my wife bolts for the bathroom like she's competing in the Nausea Olympics.

That's when I learned three key truths:

- "Morning sickness" is a scam—it hits 24/7.
- Smells are now weapons-grade.
- I should probably start eating outside.

It's Not Just the Mornings
"Morning sickness" sounds like it clocks in at 8 and clocks out at noon. Don't fall for it. This stuff hits whenever it wants—before breakfast, during a Zoom call, 20 minutes after she says she's fine. For some women, it's light and annoying. For others, it's a daily beatdown.

Her body's surging with hCG, estrogen, and every hormone in the book. Digestion slows to a crawl. Her sense of smell could rival a bloodhound's. That's not "being dramatic." It's straight-up biology.

And you? You might feel useless. You're not—you're just not in control. Which sucks, but welcome to the club. Your job here is to be the anchor, not the expert.

When It's More Than Just "Morning Sickness"
Most nausea is rough but manageable. But sometimes it crosses the line into hyperemesis gravidarum—the hard-mode version.

If she's vomiting several times a day, can't keep down water, is losing weight, or looks absolutely wrecked from doing nothing, that's when you raise the flag.

Call the OB. Ask about meds or hydration support—don't wait for her to downplay it. This isn't about "being tough." This is about staying healthy.

💡 **Dad Tip: If It Seems Bad, Speak Up**

Dehydrated, weak, or totally wrecked? Don't just wait it out. Step up and make the call.

Stuff That Actually Helps (Sometimes)

This isn't a miracle list. It's a "might help" list. Think of it like a side quest—worth trying, but no guaranteed loot.

1. **Ginger stuff**: Tea, chews, real ginger ale. But don't force it. Sometimes ginger's the MVP. Other times, it's a betrayal.
2. **Plain carbs**: Crackers, toast, dry cereal. Anything beige and boring is your friend.
3. **Cold instead of hot**: Hot food often smells like a punch in the face. Cold stuff can be a safer zone.
4. **Smell patrol**: Crack windows. Hide the trash. Tone down the cologne. Brush your teeth twice if needed. Not a joke.
5. **Frequent snacks**: Keeps her blood sugar even. Ask what works, then stock up like it's a bunker.

Nausea Moves to Memorize

When nausea hits, you don't have time for a pep talk. Here's the quick-response guide—symptoms on the left, your move on the right. Memorize it now, thank me later.

Symptom	Your Move
Sudden gag reflex	Open a window, don't ask questions.
Smells triggering barf-mode	Brush your teeth, take out trash, ditch cologne.
Too sick to talk	Quietly slide over crackers and ginger tea.
Wants food then rejects it	Say, "No problem," and reload—no pouting.
Multiple days of vomiting	Call the OB—don't wait for her to ask.

ϙ **Dad Tip**

Build a "barf kit" for the car or her side of the bed: crackers, wipes, plastic bag, water. Not glamorous—but totally clutch.

⌖ **Mini Gear List: The Anti-Nausea Starter Pack**

Not a cure, but a survival kit. Stock this gear and you'll save yourself (and her) from some of the worst moments. Bonus: you'll look like you know what you're doing.

Stuff That Helps

- Ginger chews or tea (don't force it)
- Sea-Bands (yes, goofy—but sometimes work)
- Saltines, dry cereal, or whatever she can stomach
- Plastic bags or barf bags (car and bedroom)
- Breath mints (for you—not kidding)
- A cold Sprite or electrolyte drink

Stuff That Makes It Worse

- Suggesting miracle cures from your Reddit deep dive
- Saying, "Just eat something, you'll feel better"
- Whining because she doesn't want your favorite Thai takeout
- Complaining you're bored with bland food

Cravings Are Weird. Accept It.

Cravings aren't supposed to make sense. One minute it's cheesy bread or bust. The next, she wants peanut butter and pickles but only if they're cold.

You don't have to understand cravings—you just have to support the mission.

Some cravings are about comfort. Others might be her body saying "I need salt" or "I need carbs now or I will rage." The logic isn't your job. Your job's to roll with it.

And here's the kicker—she might beg for something, then instantly hate it.

Don't argue. Don't take it personal. Just adapt and reload.

💡 **Dad Tip: Be Chill About the Food Stuff**
You're not the one barfing. Stay flexible. Don't pout. Just follow her lead on food—even if it feels like chaos.

☑ **Partner Wins: Food Survival Checklist**
Food gets weird in the first trimester. Here's how to roll with it like a pro—and what'll backfire fast.

Stuff That Actually Helps:

- Keep crackers in her bag, car, or nightstand
- Ask before reheating anything
- Offer cold drinks or ginger tea
- Carry gum or mints—if your breath is triggering her gag reflex
- Follow her food lead—even if it grosses you out

Stuff That Makes It Worse:

- Offering unsolicited fixes mid-nausea
- Complaining about limited food choices
- Making fun of cravings (unless she starts the joke)
- Acting like this phase isn't a big deal

💬 **Reflection Prompt**
What's one small way you can make food—or food avoidance—a little easier for her this week?

🎭 **Dad Sanity Check**

- What part of this food/nausea chaos is hardest for me to deal with?
- How am I reminding myself that steady beats "solutions" right now?

2.3: TALKING TO DOCTORS—HOW TO BE USEFUL WITHOUT HOVERING

I wasn't all there in those early appointments.

Not because I didn't care. It just didn't feel real yet. I showed up, sure, but I was still processing. I nodded when the doctor spoke, tossed in a few sympathetic noises—but my brain was miles away.

Later, I found myself looking up what I should've asked: "What symptoms are concerning?" "Do I really need to come to every appointment?" The internet gave me 47 conflicting answers and zero clarity.

Then my partner asked me, "What did the doctor say about the ultrasound schedule?" And I drew a complete blank. I'd tuned out—probably staring at the hand sanitizer dispenser. That sucked.

So here's the deal: I want you to do better than I did. You don't need a clipboard. You just need to be there—really be there. Pay attention. Ask. Write. You're not a guest in the waiting room—you're part of the team.

Why These Appointments Are Worth a Real Sit-In
These aren't just quick check-ins. They're permission slips, strategy sessions, and emotional pit stops. Talks about genetic tests, nutrition, and lifestyle changes are laying the foundation for your whole parental game.

When doctors throw out terms like "non-invasive screening" or "gestational diabetes," you want both of you leaving informed—not searching it online later. Your calm, curious presence keeps the train on track.

What These First Visits Actually Look Like
Here's what you'll actually run into at those early visits—so you're not blindsided.

- Paperwork and medical history. For both of you: more than you'd think.
- Bloodwork and initial tests. You might get poked too, so be ready.
- Ultrasound or Doppler check: confirm the heartbeat, identify the due date.

- Discussions—due dates, vitamins, meds, lifestyle—you both need to hear this.
- Virtual visits still count—You can't ghost just because it's on Zoom.

What She Needs From You in That Room

- An extra set of ears: Hormones, nerves, and early symptoms can fog her memory. You're the human backup drive.
- A calm presence: If she's anxious or trying not to cry, your focus helps keep things grounded.
- A question anchor: Prep with her beforehand. Even if she's quiet, have two or three questions ready.

💡 Dad Tip

Take notes—even just five bullet points can make a big difference. Not a notepad guy? Use your phone's Notes app. It's way less awkward than juggling a mini notebook—and you're more likely to actually refer back to it. Bonus: you can drop stuff straight into your shared file afterward.

Organize the Info: Save appointment notes, next steps, and your birth plan in a shared doc or folder (Docs, Notes, or whatever works for you both). That way, you're not scrambling for info when it matters.

What You Should Feel & Say to Your Doctor

It's okay if you're feeling overwhelmed or clueless. Doctors and nurses expect it—you're building a family now, not just watching.

If something's confusing, **ask**. If you don't understand something like "pelvic realignment" or "hemoglobin threshold," just say, "Can you break that down for us?"

Here are three helpful things you can say:

1. "What should I be hearing in two weeks?"
2. "If I miss one of these appointments, is that bad?"
3. "I'm here too. What can I do to help support her?"

You're not extra luggage—you're part of the load she's carrying.

What Not to Do in That Room
Quick reminder: don't be this guy.

- Don't scroll your phone like you're waiting on an Uber.
- Don't interrupt her in the middle of answering
- Don't act like this isn't your thing too.
- Don't stress about asking something that seems dumb—you won't be the first.

Appointment Prep Card: First 3 OB Visits – What to Know & Ask
Want to look like you know what's happening? Here's your cheat card for the first three OB visits.

Visit 1
- Confirm pregnancy + due date
- Submit medical history
- Ask: "Anything we should be adjusting right away?"

Visit 2
- Ultrasound/Doppler stick to hear that heartbeat
- Review any early symptoms & test results
- Ask: "What's normal to worry about—and when should we call?"

Visit 3
- Possibly another heartbeat check, weight & vitals
- Discuss screening tests or decisions coming up
- Ask: "What should we prep for next month?"

💡 Dad Tip: Treat It Like Your Appointment Too

You're not tagging along—you're in it. Ask your one or two thoughtful questions, write things down, follow up on action items, and put future appointments in your calendar too. That's how you win at this.

☑ PARTNER Wins: Appointment Survival Checklist

Here's your before, during, and after game plan for OB visits.

Before the visit

- Add it to your shared calendar
- Pack snacks, water, and her paperwork/insurance card
- Talk through both your questions—and grab a hot tip or two

During the visit

- Be the note taker
- Listen for "next steps" signals
- Make eye contact with her and the provider—don't drift off counting ceiling tiles.

After the visit

- Ask how she felt emotionally, not just medically
- Clarify anything confusing
- Offer to set reminders for the next appointment

💬 Reflection Prompt

What's one question I want to hit next appointment—about her, the baby, or my own part in this?

🐣 Dad Sanity Check

- Did I feel present or invisible last time? Why?
- Did I understand everything? If not, what's holding me back from asking?

2.4: HORMONES, HEADSPACE, AND BEING HER CALM

A few weeks into the pregnancy, I watched my wife cry... then laugh. Then apologize. Then get mad at herself for apologizing. All while I stood there holding a bagel, wondering if I was supposed to do something, nothing... or both at once.

Here's the truth no one really tells you at first: sometimes the best move is not to react. Just witness. Hold steady. Be her calm in the middle of the storm.

What's Actually Happening
She's not "overly emotional." Her body's literally rewriting itself at the cellular level. Estrogen, progesterone, and hCG are running wild. These hormones affect everything: sleep, digestion, blood sugar, anxiety, libido, even how she smells and hears things. You're not imagining it. Her senses are turned way up.

Emotionally, that hormone cocktail amps up the amygdala (your brain's threat sensor) while dialing down the prefrontal cortex (the logic filter). So everything feels more intense, more urgent, and just... more.

It's not fake—it's chemical. And it's exhausting.

Mood Swings: Not About You (Even If They Land On You)
You might be tempted to take it personally when she's sharp with you, or crying out of nowhere. But here's the mindset shift: You're the safest place she has to let the seams come loose.

It's not a punishment. It's actually a sign she trusts you enough to stop holding it together.

So when it hits, your move is simple: Don't flinch. Don't try to counter it with logic. Don't go cold or silent. Just hold space. Maybe rub her back. Maybe say nothing.

If you're thinking, "But I want to help!"—this is helping. Being a soft landing zone matters more than any perfect response.

Emotional Whiplash: Why It Happens

This is when she swings from one feeling to the next in seconds. Here's what that looks like:

- "I feel like I'm not myself."
- "I'm so excited, but also low-key freaking out."
- "I love you so much. Don't touch me."
- "This is amazing. I kind of hate this."

These aren't contradictions. They're overlapping truths showing up all at once. Think of it like overlapping browser tabs—some joyful, some scared, some still stuck on the spinning wheel.

She's not unstable. She's adapting to a major identity shift. The future just got very real, and she's carrying the weight of it—literally and emotionally.

How You Can Actually Help (Without Trying to "Fix")

So what do you actually do when it's all hitting the fan? Try this approach—low on fixing, high on support.

- **Validate without problem-solving:** "That sounds hard" goes farther than "You'll be okay."
- **Mirror calm:** If she spirals and you stay grounded, it helps pull things back down.
- **Offer help—then do it quietly:** A warm tea, her favorite socks, a refilled water bottle.
- **Notice what doesn't need a response:** Some vents just need air, not answers.
- **Make space without checking out:** Give her room when she needs it, but don't disappear.

💡 **Dad Tip**

Pay attention to what time of day her moods tend to peak. Not creepy—just strategic. If she crashes in the late afternoon, plan for quiet or extra comfort then.

☑ **Partner Wins: Low-Key Emotional Support**

Big support isn't always big gestures. Sometimes, it's just saying the one thing she needs to hear in that moment—and meaning it.

- "Want me to listen or distract you?"
- "That makes sense."
- "You're allowed to feel all of this."
- Hugs—but only if she wants one. Ask first.
- Be the one who doesn't flinch when the tears or snaps come.

---

5 Mood Shifts That Might Surprise You

Still wondering if all this is normal? Here are some emotional curveballs—and how to handle them without flinching.

Mood Shift	What It Might Sound Like	Your Move
Emotional whiplash	"I'm thrilled... and also panicking."	Nod. Validate. Stay close.
Sensory overload	"Can you stop breathing so loud?"	Respect the space—quiet counts.
Sadness for no reason	She's crying at a cereal ad.	Offer comfort, not explanations.
Sudden irritability	"Why is that spoon so loud?"	Don't take it personal. It's not.
Wanting connection... then space	"Come here. No wait, don't."	Just follow her lead. Gently.

Postpartum heads-up: These emotional swings? They can hit even harder after birth. That's normal too. It's a reminder to keep practicing presence now, before the big game.

☐ Reflection Prompt

What's one way I can create more emotional safety for her this week—without making it about me?

☺ Dad Sanity Check

- What am I not saying because I think I need to "be strong"?
- What helps me stay centered when her moods are unpredictable?

Trimester 1 Wrap-Up: Still Standing—Mostly

If you've made it this far without calling her craving weird, missing the OB appointment, or nuking leftover fish with the windows shut—you're ahead of the curve.

These first months are about learning how to stay when things get messy. About being steady when things get shaky. About ditching the fix-it reflex and getting good at just being there.

If you're starting to feel like more than a spectator—like someone who's actually in it—that's a massive win.

You're not supposed to have all the answers. Neither is she. But the fact that you're still here, still showing up, still trying? That's the real work.

So stretch your back. Recharge a bit. Maybe refill the ginger chew stash. Because Trimester Two is next.

And the baby bump? It's about to enter the chat.

PART 3

TRIMESTER 2—PLANNING, PRESSURE & KICKING INTO GEAR (MONTHS 4–6)

"Fathering is not something perfect men do,
but something that perfects the man."
—Frank Pittman

I'll be honest—Trimester 2 threw me a little.

One week it felt like nothing had changed, and the next? The bump was there. The baby was kicking. Strangers started asking questions. And somehow, I was expected to have opinions about crib colors, middle names, and whether "sage green" was too trendy.

This stretch is wild. You're still months away from holding your kid, but everything around you is shifting—your partner's body, your sleep schedule, your bank account, your brain.

For me, this was where it stopped being abstract. The baby wasn't just an idea anymore—it was real. And that meant I had to start showing up in real ways, not just saying "sounds good" from the couch.

Let's talk about what that actually looks like. What's worth caring about, what you can let go of, and how to show up now without losing your mind—or your Saturdays to building furniture with 47 screws and no words in the manual.

3.1: THE BABY BUMP IS REAL—SO IS THE PRESSURE

There was this one day—I don't even know exactly when it happened—but I looked at her and suddenly thought, Whoa. That's a real baby bump.

One week she just looked like she'd crushed a big lunch—then boom, clear belly, unmistakably pregnant.

And that's when it clicked: We're not just "having a baby" someday. It's happening now. This is real.

Before, I knew it in my head. But now? I see it. Everyone sees it. And that changes things.

One minute it's your little secret. Then the next part hits:

- Coworkers start asking when she's due.
- Your mom starts texting baby name lists.
- A stranger at the grocery store acts like her belly is public property.

This is the moment it looks real, so it suddenly feels real. And suddenly, everyone else thinks they get a say.

The Bump Brings Attention (Wanted or Not)
For your partner, that bump is both amazing and overwhelming. On a good day, it's a badge of pride—her body's growing a whole human. On a rough day, it's a magnet for comments, questions, and comparisons she didn't ask for.

She might feel radiant one minute and totally disconnected from her body the next. That doesn't mean something's wrong. It just means she's adjusting—to the new attention, to the weird body stuff, to the fact that she looks different now.

Your job? Don't assume. Ask how she feels today. Tell her she's beautiful—not just "cute pregnant," but her-her. Don't let anyone reduce her to "just the belly"—not even you.

Quick note on your own body stuff—don't be shocked if you gain a few pounds too. Sympathy weight's a thing. For some dads, it's late-night snack bonding; for others, it's feeling sluggish or self-conscious. Either way: normal. Take care of yourself the same way you're taking care of her.

You're Gonna Get Asked to "Feel It!"
Kicks start happening now. And when she grabs your hand and says, "The baby's moving!"—you're on deck.

Sometimes you'll feel it, sometimes you'll miss it—say "wow" anyway.

To you it might feel like a soft poke or a bubble. To her, it's a magic moment—one she's inviting you into. Your reaction doesn't have to be Oscar-worthy. Just be present. Be interested. Be there.

💡 **Dad Tip**
Say "Wow" every time. It's not about the words, it's about showing her you're in this. Even if it's the third time that day. Even if you're halfway through your burrito. That little "wow" tells her: I see you. I'm in this.

Dad Reframe: It's Not About Being the Hero
This isn't about swooping in with the perfect line or moment. It's about helping her feel seen, safe, and supported. That's how you win—not by fixing, but by showing up.

☑ **Partner Wins: Small Moves, Big Impact**
Want to be the guy who actually gets it right during this wild trimester? These small, easy wins go a long way.

- Ask how she feels about her body now that the bump is out
- Step in if someone touches her without asking—yep, even your mom.
- Show interest when she invites you to feel a kick or hear a new update
- Take the pic—and tell her she looks amazing.
- Remind her she's still the woman you love, not just a baby-maker

Take a second. The bump isn't just a visual—it's a mental shift for both of you.

💬 Mini-Script for Unwanted Questions:

"We're keeping some of that private, but thanks for asking."

It's simple, polite, and shuts down nosy questions about names, birth plans, or belly size without turning it into a showdown.

💬 **Reflection Prompt**

What changes am I noticing in her that I haven't mentioned yet?

What's one way I can help her feel seen—as more than a mom-to-be?

🧠 **Dad Sanity Check**

- What outside pressure is creeping in for me right now—money, family, work, expectations?
- Am I actually processing it, or pretending it's fine?

3.2: NURSERY SETUP, BABY NAMES, AND OTHER LANDMINES

At first, I thought prepping for the baby would be the fun part. Painting a room, tossing around names, maybe building a crib while cracking a beer and pretending I knew how an Allen wrench works.

And yeah, some of it is fun. But I won't lie—this stretch can come with more pressure than you expect.

Nursery setup and name-picking aren't just tasks—they're emotional minefields, and your first real co-parent test. They can go sideways fast if you're not paying attention.

Nursery Vibes and Silent Power Struggles
You might think you're just helping decorate a room. But to your partner, the nursery is this deeply personal space she's building from scratch for a person

she's literally growing inside her body. So if she's obsessing over paint swatches or crying over curtain rods—it's not about the curtain rods.

For us, it was all about green. Earthy, peaceful, gender-neutral green.

I suggested something like "adventure" or "woodland creature" as a theme. She looked at me like I'd just offered to wallpaper the crib. "Cozy plants, natural wood, and a soft rug are the theme," she said. Message received.

Here's the move: ask where you can help, and actually follow through. Don't just say "I'll hang the shelves"—do it without being reminded. And for the love of drywall, use a stud finder.

Sometimes being involved just means building the thing—and keeping quiet about throw pillows.

☑ **Dad's Nursery Task Checklist: Your quick wins right here**
Want to be useful without stepping on the "vision"? Start here.

- Use a stud finder and install wall anchors before hanging shelves or decor
- Assemble major gear early: crib, dresser, changing table
- Install outlet covers and secure cords
- Anchor furniture to walls to prevent tipping
- Set up lighting (night-light or dimmer)
- Test baby monitor placement
- Pre-stock diaper station: diapers, wipes, creams

I'll be real with you—I waited too long to put the crib together. It wasn't that the baby came early. We just had a lot going on, and I kept thinking I had more time. The crib was painted (green, of course), but still sitting in pieces when the baby arrived. We ended up using a Pack 'n Play in our room at first. It worked, and thankfully my wife didn't make it a big deal—but I knew I'd dropped the ball.

You always think you have more time—until life speeds up and the list doesn't check itself off. So if you've got a moment now? Use it. Build the thing.

Respect the Nesting Zone

Nesting isn't just a quirky behavior—it's how she contributes, and how she stays connected.

Let her lead on fundamentals like layout and style. Your role? Ask how you can help her energy flow—then execute without questioning the vision. And yes— nesting energy counts as real contribution.

Baby Names: Where Love Meets Negotiation

You'd think naming a human would be this beautiful bonding experience. Instead, it's like co-writing a screenplay where every idea gets workshopped, vetoed, and sent back for rewrites.

Name ideas came in at all hours—texts, Pinterest boards, screenshots, even random street signs. One day it was "Adelaide," the next it was "Dylan." We landed on Juniper, mostly because of a seasonal Starbucks drink. I'm not even mad—it fits.

Thing is, names are personal. Sometimes a name sounds great… until you remember your third-grade nemesis had it. That's why we came up with the 3-List System:

Name Game: The 3-List System

Picking a name can feel like choosing a tattoo for someone else's face. Don't overcomplicate it—just start here:

- Yes—names you both love
- No—hard pass, no explanation needed
- Maybe—names you're not sure about yet, but could come around to

Put the list in a shared Notes app or slap it on the fridge. Say the full name out loud—picture yelling it across a playground. Sometimes the right one picks itself.

Landmine Alert: Common Setup Fights

These setups seem simple—until they explode. Here's how to spot the common fight traps and disarm them early.

Landmine	Why it sparks a fight	Avoid it by...
Skipping crib instructions	Missed steps = frustration	Read and follow the manual together
Vetoing a name without options	Sounds dismissive and shuts dialogue	Say, "Not my favorite—what about X or Y instead?"
Pushing budget too hard	Feels like delegitimizing her choices	Acknowledge the why, offer trades (e.g., DIY vs. buy)

Dad Tip: Don't Let the Small Stuff Turn Into a Turf War

She's not just decorating—she's dreaming, nesting, coping. Your job? Stay helpful, not territorial. It's not about the perfect rug—it's about making space for your kid and your partner.

Quick Wins Checklist

Feeling the pressure? These are quick wins that show up where it counts.

- Ask: "What part of the nursery can I actually take off your plate?"
- Build the crib, the dresser, the anything—with actual instructions
- Put together a shared baby name list—with "yes," "no," and "maybe" columns.
- Don't shut down her favorite name unless you're ready to suggest five others
- Back her up when she gets excited, even if it's over wallpaper

Reflection Prompt

What's one thing she's excited about—theme, color, name—that I can support without making it about my opinion?

⊛ **Dad Sanity Check**

Where am I pushing to feel in control—and where do I need to chill out and just be a teammate?

3.3: SURVIVAL TIP #3—BUDGETING WITHOUT PANIC

There's a moment when the numbers hit you—strollers, hospital bills, twenty kinds of bottles—and your brain turns into a slot machine—diapers, car seat, formula, ding ding ding... broke.

For me, it happened in bed one night, scrolling through our registry while my wife slept. Every time I added something, I imagined our bank account screaming. I started wondering if we needed a second job just to cover swaddles.

Here's what I wish I'd realized earlier:

- You don't need it all at once.
- You don't need it all brand new.
- Most of the panic's about control, not reality.

Once I learned what actually mattered, the stress dropped fast.

The Big 3 Budget Busters

This is where the pressure usually hits your wallet—and your brain. Knowing what's coming helps you plan (and panic less):

1. **Gear:** Crib, car seat, bottles, monitor, stroller.
2. **Medical Bills:** Even with insurance, expect out-of-pocket for prenatal care, ultrasounds, delivery, and follow-ups.
3. **Time Off:** This one sneaks up. If you're taking leave (and you should), it might mean using PTO or going unpaid.

Quick note on that last one—**taking time off isn't a luxury.** It's part of showing up for your family. Even a few days here and there matters. Talk to HR now about FMLA, PTO, or state paid leave. Confusing? Yes. Worth it? Absolutely.

Spend On vs. Skip (or Wait On)

You don't need a warehouse of baby gear—just the stuff that matters. Here's what to buy now and what to chill on.

Spend On (What actually matters)	Skip or Wait (Stuff you don't need yet—or at all)
Car seat—non-negotiable	Wipe warmer
Crib or bassinet	Fancy changing table
Diapers & wipes	Designer newborn clothes
Bottles/formula/pump gear	Baby shoes
Takeout after birth	Every type of swaddle ever made

Gear We Regretted Buying

Not all gear earns its keep. Here's what flopped at our house—and what we learned from it.

- Wipe warmer (looked cool, never used)
- $300 smart swing (baby hated it)
- Fancy bottle sterilizer (sink + soap = fine)
- Designer newborn outfits (poop magnets)

Want to skip the regret pile? Ask other parents what they never used. And don't sleep on hand-me-downs—our coworker's bag of used baby stuff was a goldmine. That's how we learned zip-up onesies are king, bibs save laundry, and some baby mittens are basically scams.

Registry FOMO Is Real

Most so-called "must-haves" are just guilt-wrapped marketing pitches. You do not need a $900 stroller for a third-floor walk-up. Start with essentials. Add the rest once you meet your actual baby.

> 💡 **Dad Tip: Budget and Buy Like a Strategist, Not a Panicker**
> Borrow what you can, buy what matters, and leave room to adjust once the baby actually shows up. Set aside $200–$500 for surprise stuff—like lactation consultants, extra scans, or gear upgrades. Think of it as an "oh crap" fund.

Time Off 101: What to Ask HR

Don't wait until she's in labor to figure this out. Lock it in early—your future sleep-deprived self will thank you.

- **FMLA (Family and Medical Leave Act):** Up to 12 weeks of unpaid, job-protected leave (if you qualify). It's not paid, but your job's safe.
- **PTO (Paid Time Off):** Your vacation and sick time. Some places are flexible if you ask early.
- **State Paid Family Leave:** A bunch of states (CA, NY, NJ, WA, etc.) offer paid time off for bonding. Look it up now—not later.

You're not asking for a favor—you're making a plan to be present.

🎯 **Bonus Resource: Dad Leave Cheat Sheet**

If you're wading through HR policies and want a straight-up guide to what's actually available—including what to ask, when to take it, and where to find state-specific info—check out the Dad Leave Cheat Sheet included in the Book Bonuses mentioned in the introduction.

You don't need to memorize labor law. Just know your rights, talk to your partner, and have a plan that lets you be there when it counts.

☑ **PARTNER Wins: Quick Budget Checklist**

Trying to be useful without adding to the stress? Start with these budget-friendly wins.

- Make a simple baby budget (shared doc or app)
- Prioritize safety gear and feeding basics
- Ask HR about all leave options
- Hunt used gear in local groups/marketplaces
- Don't bulk-buy until you know your baby likes it

💬 **Reflection Prompt**

- What's one money worry I haven't said out loud yet?
- What's something I can buy used, borrow, or wait on?

🧠 **DAD Sanity Check**

- What financial pressure is real, and what's just noise?
- How can I protect our peace and our wallet?

Bottom line: You're not building a theme park. You're building a family. Keep your cool, plan smart, and remember—your presence is worth more than any purchase.

3.4: ANATOMY SCANS & MILESTONE MOMENTS

I missed our first ultrasound.

Work conflict. Bad timing. Still one of my biggest regrets. She texted me the image—a blurry little blob on a black screen—and I stared at it, willing myself to feel something. But I wasn't there. I didn't hear the heartbeat. I didn't hold her hand.

Weeks later, we booked a private scan just so I could see for myself. The tech handed us a stuffed bear with our daughter's heartbeat recorded inside. That bear lived on our bed until she was born. Years later, it's still in her room. That's when it hit me—this isn't just a pregnancy. This is my kid.

Ultrasounds aren't just medical check-ins—they're memory makers, if you're actually there for them.

What the Anatomy Scan Checks

The anatomy scan usually goes down between **18–22 weeks,** and it's the big one. The tech or doctor checks your baby's:

- Brain and skull
- Face and limbs
- Heart and its four chambers
- Organs—kidneys, stomach, bladder
- Spine and bones
- Placenta placement and amniotic fluid
- Overall size and due date

This is also when you can find out the sex of the baby if you want to. Or you can ask them to write it down, seal it in an envelope, and pretend you'll wait—good luck with that.

The scan takes 30–45 minutes, longer if your baby decides to play hide-and-seek. Sometimes you have to come back to get better images. It's totally normal.

Questions You Can Ask the Doctor

If you want to feel connected and in the loop, here are a few questions worth asking:

- "Is everything measuring on track?"
- "What should we watch for at the next scan?"
- "Where's the placenta positioned—and does that matter later on?"

You're not overstepping. You're showing up.

How It Might Hit You

Watching that screen is wild—tiny arms stretching, maybe a yawn, a heartbeat that can stop you mid-breath.

You could feel overwhelmed, amazed, or even numb. That's all normal. Don't fake a tear for her sake. Just be there, fully there. Watch your baby. Ask the questions. Take it in.

Later that night, try writing something down: just a sentence or two. "I saw our baby move today." That's a line you'll want to remember.

💡 **Dad Tip: Moment Locker.**
Jot down one sentence in your phone notes or on a sticky note that night. Something like, "He scratched his face with the tiniest hand I've ever seen." Save it in your memory box—or just keep it for future-you. These tiny time capsules hit different later.

And If You Don't Feel The Magic?

Not every parent feels instantly bonded during ultrasounds. If you're more confused than connected right now, that's okay. You're not broken—you're adjusting. Give it time. Keep showing up. The feelings will catch up.

If Something Comes Up

Sometimes they see something that's not 100% clear—like a measurement that needs double-checking, or a structure they couldn't get a good view of. It doesn't mean something's wrong. But yeah, the room can go quiet. Your heart might race—and that's normal.

If that happens:

- **Stay calm.** Deep breath.
- **Grab her hand.** Let her know you're not going anywhere.
- **Don't press the tech for answers**—they can't give a diagnosis.
- **Wait for the doctor.** Ask the questions then.

You're not there to fix anything. You're there to show up and hold steady. That's exactly what she needs.

♀ Dad Tip: Be Curious, Not a Know-It-All

Bring a notebook or open your Notes app. Write down stuff to look up later. Don't act like you've got it all figured out. Curiosity is a dad superpower.

Ultrasound Moments

These small moves help mark the moment—and might mean more than you think down the road:

- Take a photo of the screen (if they let you)
- Save the printout
- Write down the date
- Label the fridge magnet

It might look like static now, but one day you'll recognize that blurry profile anywhere.

♡ Reflection Prompt

What did I see, hear, or feel during that ultrasound that I don't want to forget?

🐣 Dad Sanity Check

- What surprised me, and what do I want to ask next time—even if I'm nervous?

Wrap-Up: You're past the halfway mark.

That blurry ultrasound image? That first kick? That name you keep testing in your head? All real.

This stretch hits different—you're not just planning anymore. You're starting to believe it. You're picturing the face behind the movement. You're showing up not just for her, but for someone you haven't even met.

You've been building skills without realizing it—tuning in, adjusting, stepping up. That foundation? It's going to matter more than ever in the next stretch.

Next up: the home stretch. Hospital bags, late-night practice contractions, big emotions, big choices.

Time to stay sharp.

PART 4

TRIMESTER 3—GO TIME GETS REAL (MONTHS 7-9)

"Never is a man more of a man than when he is the father of a newborn."
—Matthew McConaughey, Greenlights

Third trimester hit harder than I expected.

My wife was sore, swollen, and barely sleeping. I was watching the calendar like it was ticking down to something huge—because it was. Even with a scheduled induction on the books, I felt this tension creeping in. Like I should be doing more, but wasn't sure what.

This stretch is where everything tightens: the belly, the timelines, the margin for error. It's also where your role sharpens. You're not guessing anymore—you're stepping in, calmly, clearly, and probably with snacks.

You don't need to have all the answers. But you do need to be the guy who holds steady when she's exhausted and everything feels a little unglued.

Let's walk through what that actually looks like—month by month, moment by moment.

4.1: HOSPITAL BAG PACKING—YES, YOU TOO

Here's how I blew it the first time: my wife followed a detailed hospital packing checklist weeks in advance. She even highlighted the "dad" section for me. I glanced at it, tossed it on the table, and figured I'd pack when it got closer. Like the crib, I figured I had time. And—like the crib—I never got around to it.

Fast forward to the middle of the night, in the hospital, watching her breathe through contractions while I realized I didn't have clean underwear, a charger, or even a damn toothbrush. I felt useless. Then I had to leave—leave—because I forgot half the stuff that would've helped both of us through that night.

Second kid? I was a different man. Bag packed, chargers coiled, snacks locked in. Didn't make that mistake again.

So here's your cheat sheet—not just for stuff, but for mindset. You're not packing like you're tagging along—you're packing like you're a teammate, a co-pilot, and the guy who might be sleeping upright in a stiff vinyl chair while trying to remember what the nurse just said about dilation.

What to Bring So You're Not Useless When It's Go Time
So what actually goes in your bag? Here's a breakdown—your stuff, her comfort gear, and the little extras that make a big difference.

Your Essentials (Yes, Yours):

- Change of clothes (at least two shirts, underwear, socks)
- Hoodie or zip-up—those hospital rooms swing cold
- Toothbrush, deodorant, floss (yes, floss), and basic toiletries. You'll thank yourself.
- Phone and charger—extra-long cable if you've got one.
- Refillable water bottle
- Headphones or earbuds (for music, podcasts, mental breaks)
- Something to sleep on if allowed—a pillow or compact blanket beats hospital couch upholstery
- Meds you take daily (don't assume they'll have 'em)

Snack Survival Kit:

- High-protein, no-refrigeration snacks (trail mix, jerky, granola bars)
- Gum or mints (for your breath, and for hers if she wants it during labor)
- Cash or coins for vending machines—some still live in the past.

Her Comfort Boosters (That She Might Forget):

- Hair ties, lip balm, comfy socks, lotion
- Her favorite snacks and a cozy sweater
- Printed copy of the birth plan—if she's made one.
- Extra-long phone charger for her too
- Hospital paperwork, ID, insurance info

Your Job Extras:

- Notepad or phone app for questions and updates
- Text list of people to notify when the baby arrives
- Small duffel bag for hauling home diapers, mesh underwear, and random hospital freebies like extra pads or wipes

---

Last-Minute Grab Items

Here's the lightning-round stuff people always forget—grab these before heading out the door.

- Phone and charger (extralong cable if you've got one)
- Wallet & ID (yes, you'll need them)
- Glasses or contacts kit
- House or car keys
- Hospital parking pass (if needed)

⚙ **Bonus Resource: Printable Hospital Bag Checklist**

Need a readymade version of this? There's a downloadable Hospital Bag Checklist in the Book Bonuses linked via QR code in the Introduction. Print it, stuff it in your bag, and check off as you go—no improvising in the middle of contractions.

💡 **Dad Tip: Pack Like You're Gonna Sleep on a Vinyl Chair**

Hospital time stretches—long waits, bursts of chaos… then more waiting. Having what you need won't just make you more comfortable—it will make you a steadier presence when things get real.

☑ **Partner Wins: Small Moves That Say "I've Got You"**
Want to show her you're not just along for the ride? These moves say "I've got you" louder than any birth plan.

- Pack early, so she never has to remind you.
- Toss in her comfort extras: snacks, cozy socks, long charger.
- Slip in a small surprise: her favorite candy, a sweet note, or a calming playlist.
- Have paperwork and IDs ready. Be the guy who handles the boring stuff.
- Double-check chargers and snacks. Hunger and dead phones are real.
- Bring an extra bag. Hospital freebies are no joke.

💭 **Reflection Prompt**
What's one thing I can pack that proves I'm thinking ahead—not just about me, but about her?

🧠 **Dad Sanity Check**
- If I had to head straight from work to the hospital, would I be ready?
- What's one simple thing I can prep now that will make labor day go smoother later?

4.2: SURVIVAL TIP #4—BIRTH PLANS & WHY DADS SHOULD CARE

When I first heard "birth plan," I figured my wife would handle it while I just held snacks, tissues, and her hand.

Then we had a planned induction—and she handed me that birth plan again while we sat in triage. She told me, pointblank: "I want it all done—pain meds, monitoring, everything." I read it over, told her I got it.

Fast-forward, and things got hectic. The baby showed distress during induction, and they wheeled her out for an emergency C-section. It was scary. I wasn't allowed in the OR. I was outside, clutching that plan, watching people wait for news I couldn't deliver. I needed that plan—in my hands, in my mind—to stay grounded while I waited.

That's exactly why this matters. This isn't about controlling how the birth goes: it's about knowing what she wants, so when everything moves lightning fast, you're not lost. You're not left flailing and hoping for the best. You're ready.

What a Birth Plan Actually Covers

It's not a script—it's a playbook. Stuff changes. But having a plan means you're not making big calls in the heat of the moment without a clue what she wanted.

Here's what it usually covers:

- **Pain management:** Epidural ASAP, or hold off as long as possible?
- **Delivery vibe:** Lights low? Music? No crowd?
- **Who's in the room:** Doula, family, just you?
- **Interventions:** When are inductions, forceps, or meds okay?
- **C-section:** If it goes that way, what matters—partner in the OR, delayed cord clamping, skin-to-skin?
- **After birth:** Who cuts the cord, when to bathe, how to feed?

She might have it figured out already. Or not. Either way, your job is to know it—and back it up when things get loud, fast, or sideways. Birth plans aren't about control. They're about making sure she gets a say, even when she can't say it out loud. (The Mayo Clinic backs that up too.)

⌖ Bonus Resource: Birth Plan Snapshot

Want a quick visual version of the key decisions? We've got you. The printable **Birth Plan Snapshot** is available in the Book Bonuses linked via the QR code in the Introduction. It's a one-pager you can fill out together—or just keep handy in your bag or phone for go-time.

♀ Dad Tip: Learn It, Know It, Be It

You don't need to memorize her plan like a script—but you do need to carry it with you. So when things jump off and decisions fly, you're not searching for answers—you're delivering them with confidence.

Why This Matters—for Both of You

Birth is unpredictable. A calm team member with her wishes in mind can make all the difference. If questions get thrown your way while she's mid-contraction—or rushed off to an OR—knowing the plan gives you clarity instead of panic.

And if the plan changes? That's okay. In the end, flexibility is the plan. Just ask, "Sounds like that's not what you wanted—what do you want now?" And keep being that voice in her corner.

Reminder: Plans Can Change

If the plan shifts—because the baby has other ideas or things move fast—that's not failure. That's parenting. You adjust, support, and keep showing up. That is the plan.

☉ Mini-Guide: Dad Role at the Hospital

You're not just moral support—you're the one who speaks up when she can't. Here's how to step into that role without steamrolling anyone:

- **Know the plan:** Keep it handy. You're the real-time reference.
- **Read the room:** If she's in pain and being brushed off, say, "She's still hurting, can we talk pain options again?"
- **Ask, don't assume:** If things change fast, ask her, "Is this what you want now?" Then echo her voice.
- **Stay steady:** Your calm tone and steady presence can help de-escalate moments when staff is rushing or unclear.
- **Repeat the key line**—"She'd like [insert wish] if possible, can we make that happen?"

If You Can't Be in the Room (Emergency OR Situations)

- Ask the nurse: "What's happening now?" Stay calm and informed.
- Keep talking to her if you can—even by phone.
- Ask how long the procedure might take, and what you can do.
- When you're back with her, simply say, "I was out here holding it down."

You're not sidelined—you're still the steady one she needs.

☑ **Partner Wins: Actions You Can Take Today**

Want to be the guy who's ready, not just present? These small moves make a big impact when the big day comes.

- Ask if she wants to build a birth plan together
- Discuss the tough stuff—pain meds, interventions, and what the what-ifs might look like
- Save it in a shared phone doc, print a copy, or both
- Admit what you're not sure about—and ask her what to do in those scenarios
- Keep the plan accessible—like a quarterback calling a play

💡 **DAD Tip: Calm Beats Loud**

Advocating doesn't mean shouting—it means holding the line when she can't, and asking the right questions at the right time.

💬 **Reflection Prompt**
- What part of labor or delivery do I still feel shaky about?
- What question do I need answered to feel like her solid backup?

Remember, no birth goes perfectly to plan—but your presence does.

🤯 **Dad Sanity Check**
- Do I actually know her wishes—or just what sounds good?
- If things go off-script, can I adjust without losing focus or freaking out?

When it counts, you want your calm—not confusion—in your pocket. That checklist? It's not just for show. It's part of showing up.

4.3: SLEEP NOW. SERIOUSLY.

By the last trimester, sleep drains faster than a bad battery—and it doesn't matter which one of you's technically the parent-to-be. My wife was up all night: bathroom breaks every hour, midnight cravings, pillow adjustments that took thirty minutes. Meanwhile, I was halfway awake—tensing at each creak or sigh—not quite asleep and not fully present.

That's not just your sleep slipping; it's your team's rest. And it matters.

Why Sleep Now Sets the Tone
You can't stockpile sleep for later—but you can stop sabotaging it now. This phase is your last shot at semi-decent rest, and trust me, it matters.

- Sleep debt stacks up fast: One rough night is fine. Five in a row? You're foggy, short-fused, and way less helpful.
- Her body's in overdrive: Hormones, swelling, belly acrobatics—she's already losing sleep. Don't add to it.
- You're her support system: Middle-of-the-night snack runs and pillow swaps aren't glamorous. They're clutch.

How to Build Sleep Fortitude (Before the Baby Arrives)
Here's how to bunker your sleep resilience before things go wild.

- **Pre-labor routine:** Set a nightly "wind-down." Dim the lights, shut off big screens 30 minutes before bed, skip loud TV shows. Treat it like you're stepping onto the field together.
- **On-duty hydration and snacks:** Keep her ice water and a snack tray within reach, so you're not stumbling around at 2 a.m.
- **Pillow command center:** Become an expert at positioning pillows, towel rolls—whatever helps her snooze. You'll earn MVP status.
- **Low-key nighttime handoff:** One night do the bedtime dishes, the next she does them. Train your brain: rest is a shared game plan, not a solo win.
- **Own your downtime:** Naps aren't weak moves—they're strategic. A 20-minute reset mid-day can make all the difference when nighttime hits.

Sleep Strategy Isn't Just a Vibe, It's a Conversation

Here's what nobody tells you—sometimes the best way to support each other's rest is to sleep apart. Yeah, it sounds weird at first. But if her tossing, turning, or midnight bathroom parade keeps you both in zombie mode? Talk about sleeping in different rooms temporarily—or even just a night or two a week.

This isn't about "separate lives." It's about preserving energy when your team needs it most.

- Set the tone early—say, "Hey, if we're wrecked from waking each other up, want to rotate who gets the couch or guest room?"
- Trade off wake-up duties: One handles the 2 a.m. snack mission, the other gets solid rest—then switch.

It's not a failure—it's a playbook adjustment.

Couples Sleep Map (Final Weeks Game Plan)

Still awake? Here's how you and your partner can tag team rest in the home stretch.

- **Weeknight chill duty**—one of you takes the couch every third night; the other handles midnight snack and bathroom runs.
- **Weekend reset** – Alternate guest-room nights (Friday through Saturday) so both can wake up refreshed Sunday.

Put it in your shared calendar or on the fridge—it turns intention into habit.

🗩 **Script: "It's not a split—it's just smart planning."**
Say, "Hey, what if we rotated the couch or guest room so we both get real rest before the baby storm hits?

Totally a team move.

61

Dad Nap Power Move

Squeeze in a 20–30 minute reset nap: during her doc appointment, your lunch break, or early evening before dinner prep. Treat it like a timeout, not laziness. Those mini-resets build reserve for 3 a.m. feedings and freakouts.

💡 **Dad Tip: Sleep Equals Sanity. Trading rest keeps you both steady.**
These aren't romantic gestures—they're survival moves. And they build habits that'll carry you through late night feedings and early growth spurts without crashing and burning.

☑️ **Quick Cheat Sheet**

You don't need a perfect plan—just a few real moves. Here's the short version.

- Kick off a nightly wind-down routine (dim lights, screens off, low-key vibes)
- Take over bedtime setup—pillows, snacks, lights, the works
- Schedule separation nights (guest room, couch, call it a reset—not a retreat)
- Build in naps—even if they feel optional, they're fuel for the long haul

---

💬 **REFLECTION Prompt**
- What's draining our rest the most right now—and how can I take one thing off her plate this week?
- If we had to protect one good night of sleep each, what would that plan look like?

🧠 **Dad Sanity Check**
- Am I pretending I'm good when I'm just spent?
- What's one swap (chores, sleeping space, bedtime help) that can give us both 2 more hours of rest this week?

Sleep isn't just comfort—it's training. The habits you build now are your core reserves. They cushion the next phase: late-night feeds, sniffles, sunrise smiles.

So step in, step up, and rest—with intention. You're about to run the wildest marathon yet.

You're standing at the edge of the jump. All the reading, all the checklists, all the "wait, what is that?" moments—they've led here. You might still feel unprepared. That's normal. But if you've been showing up, paying attention, and trying your best to be present? You're more ready than you think.

No one's expecting perfect. But when it all goes sideways, silent, or loud at 3 a.m., she's going to look at you. You just have to be there, really there.

4.4: MONTH-BY-MONTH SURVIVAL GUIDE

You've already tackled hospital bags, sleep, birth plans—the works. But when your brain's fried and you're up at 2 a.m. thinking, "Wait…what's happening this month again?"—you need it plain and simple.

That's what this is: your no-fluff, month-by-month survival guide. Real quick hits. Just the stuff that matters.

Some of it echoes earlier chapters—but now it's all in one place. Think of it like your map for the road ahead. One glance and you know where you are, and what's coming next.

📅 MONTH 1 – THE INVISIBLE START

What's Happening
- The embryo is implanting and hCG levels are rising—no belly yet, but early symptoms begin.
- She may feel crampy, bloated, emotional, or exhausted.

What You Might Be Feeling
- It's surreal. You've got a pregnancy in the works, but it doesn't feel real yet.
- Anxiety about miscarriages and whether the pregnancy is really happening.

How You Can Help
- Sit through her first OB appointment. Help prep questions.
- Set up shared calendar and notes app like you learned in Part 1.

💡 **Dad Tip: Check in daily**
"How are you feeling today?" Even if the answer's "same—tired."

💬 **Reflection Prompt**
Do I feel present or detached? What one thing can I do to show up more?

☑ **Quick Wins**
- Download a pregnancy app and invite her to share progress.
- Stock the pantry with her comfort snacks: crackers, ginger ale, decaf tea.
- Ask: "Want me to track appointments and notes?"

📅 MONTH 2 – MOOD & BODY ROLLERCOASTER

What's Happening
- Hormones are on overload—nausea, weird cravings, fatigue, mood swings—and still no visible bump.

What You Might Be Feeling
- Useless watching her feel terrible. You want to fix it.
- Guilt if your emotional state isn't 100% fully bonded yet.

How You Can Help
- Help with a "barf kit" (crackers, wipes, plastic bag) for the sofa or car.
- Take over trash, cooking, chores so she rests more.
- Use your phone-notes to track what helps her feel better.

Create a "Nausea Moves" sheet and stick it on the fridge.

💬 **Reflection Prompt**

What's hardest for me to manage when she's feeling sick? How can I make that less rough?

☑ **Quick Wins**

- Buy ginger chews, SeaBands, a go-to snack she can eat
- Ope n the car window, hide the trash, double brush teeth.
- Ask her: "What's worst right now—and is there one thing I can fix?"

📅 MONTH 3 – BUILDING THE GAME PLAN

What's Happening

- Pregnancy is more visible—not in bump yet, but symptoms may begin to ease.
- You're closer to the end of the first trimester—appointments, screening tests.

What You Might Be Feeling

- A little relief, but still anxious about "how this all ends."
- Pressure to do something—but buying gear isn't the same as giving support.

How You Can Help

- Build the "Early Dad Game Plan" from Parts 1 (shared calendar, app, snack station).
- Draft a simple shared notes doc for doctor questions and birth plan basics.

💡 **Dad Tip**

Set up your weekly ritual: a 15minute chat + walk to keep the emotional connection alive.

💬 **Reflection Prompt**

What little ritual could keep us grounded through Week 13 and beyond?

☑ **Quick Wins**

- Invite her to pick one snack for your next grocery run.
- Share one funny/encouraging text midweek ("You're doing better than you think.")
- Confirm your shared folder has calendar, notes, birthplan draft.

📅 ## MONTH 4 – THE BUMP SHOWS UP

What's Happening

- She's showing now. You're not imagining that bump.
- Energy might return—but body changes keep coming.

What You Might Be Feeling

- A shift—people ask you about the pregnancy now.
- Pressure to "be useful," even if you're still unsure how.

How You Can Help

- Take bump pics (with her okay). It's a win when she feels seen.
- Get serious about the baby budget and gear basics—see Part 2.

💡 **Dad Tip**

Keep your bag packed too. Baby ready isn't just pink onesies—it's emotional backup.

What helps me feel more connected to the baby—even before they're born?

☑ **Quick Wins**

- Clean out your trunk to make room for eventual baby hauls.
- Set a reminder to check her prenatal appointment dates.
- Ask: "What's changed physically this month that I don't see?"

📅 ## MONTH 5 – SOUND ON, BABY IN

What's Happening

- You may hear the heartbeat. Baby's moving. The anatomy scan is coming.
- You're halfway there, which feels both fast and slow.

What You Might Be Feeling

- Excited, but nervous to get it wrong.
- Bonding more with the idea of being a dad, not just a partner.

How You Can Help

- Be at the anatomy scan. Ask questions. Be fully present.
- Write down what hit you after big milestones.

💡 **Dad Tip**
Ask what she needs this week—and follow through.

💬 **Reflection Prompt**
What do I want to remember about this phase five years from now?

☑ **Quick Wins**

- Download that heartbeat audio if you can—she'll play it over and over.
- Practice saying the baby's name out loud—if you've picked one.
- Begin mapping out your leave options—even if dates aren't set yet.

🗓 MONTH 6 – THE PLANNING PHASE KICKS IN

What's Happening

- Baby is growing fast. Her back might hurt. Braxton Hicks might show up.
- Registry, nursery, birth plan, and classes come into view.

What You Might Be Feeling

- Slightly overwhelmed—like you're gearing up for a big day without the playbook.
- More emotionally "in it" than before—and that's a good sign.

How You Can Help

- Colead the registry build. It's not "her list"—it's your squad gear.
- Help draft or carry the birth plan (see 4.2).

💡 **Dad Tip**

Be the calm one when baby talk takes over—someone's gotta keep it grounded.

💬 **Reflection Prompt**

Am I treating this like a team effort—or just a supporting role?

☑ **Quick Wins**

- Attend one birth class or online course together—then debrief like it's postgame.
- Print out or save the Book Bonus birth plan snapshot.
- Offer one surprise comfort move: warm towel, foot rub, her favorite snack prepped.

📅 MONTH 7 – THIRD TRIMESTER BEGINS

What's Happening

- Baby's packing on pounds, kicks get stronger, sleep gets harder.
- You might be hearing "wow, almost there!"—a lot.

What You Might Be Feeling

- Anxious excitement. Like you're waiting for a game that doesn't have a kickoff time.
- Stretched thin at work, home, mentally.

How You Can Help

- Be the sleep support squad (see 4.3). Snacks, water, midnight pillow patrol.
- Double down on emotional check-ins—ask how she's doing without needing to fix it.

☑ **Quick Wins**

- Prep a "couch nap" plan and trade-off sleep duties.
- Check car seat installation. Don't wing this one.
- Say out loud, "You don't have to do this alone."

💡 **Dad Tip**

Make rest a team strategy. Not just hers—yours too.

💬 **Reflection Prompt**

What part of this final stretch is hardest to say out loud?

📅 MONTH 8 – GO TIME VIBES, NO BABY YET

What's Happening
- Baby drops lower. Braxton Hicks increase. Nesting instincts hit hard.
- Hospital bag time. Leave paperwork. Name finalization.

What You Might Be Feeling
- Urgency—with no clear action.
- Hyperaware of time, even if nothing's "happening."

How You Can Help
- Pack your own hospital bag (see 4.1). For real this time.
- Finalize the logistics: leave, backup childcare (if needed), emergency numbers.
- Don't joke about "she could pop any minute" unless she starts it.

💡 **Dad Tip**

Do the unsexy prep work now. It's like setting the stage before the main event.

💬 **Reflection Prompt**

What's one practical thing I can take off her plate this week?

🗓 MONTH 9 – FINAL COUNTDOWN

What's Happening

- Full term. Could be days or weeks.
- Baby's head down (hopefully). Every cramp might feel like the one.

What You Might Be Feeling

- Antsy. On edge. Scared to leave your phone in the bathroom.
- Ready, and also totally not ready.

How You Can Help

- Be the calm. Be the driver. Be the "let's breathe through this" guy.
- Get sleep where you can. You're about to cross into New Game+ mode.

💡 Dad Tip

Keep her spirits up without dismissing the hard stuff. "This sucks, but I've got you" beats "Just a few more days" every time.

💬 Reflection Prompt

How do I want to show up when labor starts—emotionally, physically, mentally?

☑ **Quick Wins**

- Load up your gas tank. Seriously.
- Plan your "first baby text" list—names, contact order.
- Pick your playlist for the drive or the delivery room—seriously.

💬 **Final Reflection Prompt**

What kind of partner and dad do I want to be in the first week after birth—and what's one thing I can do to move in that direction now?

🎯 **Bonus Resource: Month-by-Month Survival Guide**

You'll find the printable version in the Book Bonuses—QR code's in the Introduction. Stick it on the fridge, save it to your phone, or keep it some-where you'll actually check.

You don't have to memorize it. Just know where it is. Each month will bring something new, weird, or hard. Keep checking in—on her, on yourself, on the plan—and you'll be the dad you want to be.

Remember: don't aim for perfect. Aim for present.

Wrap-Up: You just made it through the full run—three trimesters, start to finish.

From the first test to the final push, you showed up. That's the job. That's the win.

Not because you nailed every diaper decision or knew what to say when her favorite clothes didn't fit and it broke her a little—but because you stayed in it. Even when it got weird. Or hard. Or boring.

You've built tools. Gained emotional muscle. Picked up wins. Learned from misses. And you've got a whole new respect for what it means to be a partner—and a dad.

Take a breath. You earned it.

Next stop: baby in arms.

📢 Quick Favor from One Dad to Another

If you've gotten a laugh, a useful tip, or just a little more confidence from what you've read so far—could you take 30 seconds to leave a quick review?

It helps other first-time dads find this guide, and it keeps small, independent authors like me going.

(You can leave it at Amazon.com—or wherever you bought the book.)

Thanks, man. Now—back to the good stuff.

PART 5

LABOR & DELIVERY—GAME TIME

"Being a dad isn't just about eating a huge bag of gummy bears while your wife gives birth. It means being comfortable with the word hero."
—Ryan Reynolds

We had a scheduled induction. No mad dash to the hospital, no guessing if this was "it." And I was grateful for that. Still, even with the plan locked in, I was on edge. Bags were packed. My mind was racing.

Because once labor kicks off—planned or not—everything shifts.

My brother-in-law? Whole different story. They went to the hospital three times before it was actually go-time on the fourth. That kind of uncertainty messes with your head.

No matter how it starts, this is the stretch where everything gets real. You don't need to be a hero. You just need to stay present, stay steady, and show up when it counts.

Let's talk about how.

5.1: WHAT TO EXPECT FROM LABOR (AND HOW NOT TO PASS OUT)

Most guys freak out here—which is why we keep it calm and the game plan clear. Here's what you need to know.

The Stages of Labor—Simplified

Forget Hollywood—here's the real play-by-play:

- Early Labor (Crawling Pace)
  - Contractions are mild and spread out.
  - Most of this happens at home—your job is to keep her calm, hydrated, and distracted.
  - You'll probably wonder, "Is this it?" Yeah—it is.
- Active Labor (Gearing Up)
  - Contractions get stronger, closer, and longer.
  - This is when you close the distance—hand on her back, a quiet "you've got this."
  - Be helpful, not hovering.
- Transition (Storm Mode)
  - The hardest part. Intense, fast contractions.
  - It's short, but brutal.
  - She'll need you steady—even if, inside, you're quietly losing it.
- Delivery (Game Time)
  - She's pushing. You're breathing with her, cheering her on.
  - You might see everything. You might cry. You might even blank out for two seconds—then bounce back. All okay.

How Long It Might Take

Short answer: it'll take longer than you think.

Even "quick" labor is still hours. Early labor can stretch for a day. Active labor and delivery? Another 6–12 hours, easy. Bring snacks. Charge your phone. Stay off social media—unless she calls for a distraction.

Pain Management That Doesn't Suck

You're not the doula, but you can still play defense. Here's what helps:

- Deep, steady breathing—match her pace.
- Counter-pressure—firm hands on her back or hips during contractions

- Ice chips and sips of water—simple, but clutch.
- Cool washcloths, music, lip balm—little things go a long way.
- Your steady energy—it's contagious.

Support Without Hovering

Staying close without crowding her is a real skill—here's how to support without overstepping.

- Offer, don't insist. Ask "Want water?" not "Drink more."
- Stay in reach, not in her face. Let her guide how close you are.
- Keep calm energy—if you're wound up, she feels it.
- If she signals you to step back, do it—just stay emotionally present.

When Labor Doesn't Go to Plan

You might be expecting a natural, slow build to that big "push" moment. But labor has plot twists. Here's how to stay grounded:

Induction vs. Natural Labor

Not everyone gets the "movie version" where her water breaks and it's straight to the hospital. Some births are scheduled. Especially if there's a medical risk, timing concern, or the hospital wants to keep things controlled.

When we had our induction during the COVID wave, everything was planned… until it wasn't. Baby went into distress, and the team tried every position and adjustment to stabilize things. Nothing worked. My wife was wheeled into an emergency C-section, and I wasn't allowed in. I waited alone. That sucked.

But because we'd talked through her birth plan ahead of time, I could stay calm—for her, and for me.

Heads-up: Inductions often start slow, then ramp up fast. Natural labor feels less predictable, but either one can change direction in a heartbeat. Your role? Simple—stay flexible.

Vaginal vs. C-Section (Planned or Emergency)

About one in three U.S. births are C-sections (some planned, some emergencies). Here's the quick view:

- Vaginal birth: You're likely beside her, coaching, breathing, holding legs, maybe tearing up when you see your kid for the first time.
- C-section: It's surgery. Bright lights, fast pace, and a sterile setup. You might be allowed in; you might not. Either way, you're her post-op support—bringing water, holding her hand, and being there while she recovers.

Don't lock in on one "ideal." However it goes down, be there for her.

What You'll See in the Room (and Why It Feels So Intense)

If you're squeamish, overwhelmed, or just unsure what to expect—that's normal. Better to know now than freeze later.

- Machines, lights, beeping monitors—it can feel like a spaceship.
- A rotating cast of nurses, doctors, and techs—some amazing, some abrupt.
- Your partner might cry, snap, or go silent. It's not about you—that's just labor.

What Not to Do During Labor

Even with good intentions, it's easy to mess up the vibe—here's what not to do when things get intense.

- Don't ask for snacks mid-contraction.
- Don't say, "Wow, this is taking forever."
- Don't live-text your fantasy football league—or any group chat, for that matter.
- Don't get defensive if she snaps—it's not about you.
- Don't try to fix pain with logic—just hold space and breathe with her.

Around week 39, you might hear, "I just want this baby OUT." That's normal—and here's what that phase often looks like.

The "Let's Get This Baby Out" Phase

By full-term, there's a good chance your partner will feel done. Like, done-done. She might be looking up home remedies or walking stairs like it's her job. Here's what people try—with mixed results:

- Long walks
- Spicy food
- Bouncing on an exercise ball
- Nipple stimulation—yep, that's a thing
- Sex—if she's up for it. Prostaglandins plus oxytocin equals potential contractions
- Acupressure or massage

⚠ Important

Check with her provider before trying anything stronger—like castor oil or herbal teas. And never push her into it. If she wants to walk the mall, walk with her. If she'd rather nap? That's just as valid.

⚡ Dad Tip

Be the calm in the chaos. You're not the coach—you're the pit crew. Keep her steady, hydrated, and focused.

Say less. Do more.

- Don't freeze. Don't fix. Just be there.
- Not sure what she needs? Stay close. Make eye contact. That's enough.

⟳ Dad Sanity Check

- What about labor freaks you out?
- Who can you talk to before go-time?
- What habits can you build now to stay steady later?

☑ **Quick Cheat Sheet**

When it's go-time, here's the no-panic checklist that'll keep you steady.

- Learn the labor stages—and what you can actually do in each
- Keep her breathing steady—use your own breath to guide hers
- Be the bag guy, the key guy, the charger guy—so she's not thinking about it
- Track contractions early—use an app, don't guess
- Bring no extra drama. Zero. None.

💬 **Reflection Prompt**

What's one part of labor or fatherhood that secretly scares you—and what would it take to face it instead of stuffing it away?

This is the level-up moment. You're not on the sidelines anymore—you're in it. It won't go perfectly. That's fine. What matters is how you respond when it gets intense. Stay grounded. Stay close. And whatever happens—be the calm in the chaos.

5.2: HOSPITAL, BIRTH CENTER, OR HOME— WHAT'S YOUR ROLE IN EACH?

Where your kid's born isn't just a location—it sets the tone. Each setting brings its own vibe, rhythm, and curveballs.

Hospital, Home, or Birth Center: What's the Dad Role?

You might be hospital-bound. You might be staying home. Or maybe you're rolling into a birth center with string lights and a curated playlist.

Wherever your kid makes their debut, your role flexes with the setting—but the mission stays the same: stay steady, stay useful, and don't be the guy asking where to park during a contraction.

- **Hospital Birth:** Clinical, structured, tech-heavy. Your job? Be the calm anchor. You're helping her feel human in a space that feels all machine.

Let the OBs and nurses run point—but stay sharp, and speak up when she needs backup.

- **Birth Center:** The cozy middle ground. Feels like home, usually midwife-led. You'll be more hands-on—massage, counterpressure, whispering encouragement while quietly losing your mind. Be ready to assist.

- **Home Birth:** You're in it—all the way. You're setting the mood, filling the tub, guarding the vibe. You might be catching the baby or steadying her through contractions. The midwife or doula leads, but you're co-piloting this thing.

Birth Setting Snapshot

Different birth settings change the vibe—but not your job. Here's the quick breakdown.

Setting	Dad Role	Environment	Who Runs Point
Hospital	Advocate, calm anchor	Structured, clinical	OB or Nurses
Birth Center	Physical and emotional support	Cozy, midwife-led	Midwife
Home Birth	Active participant, setup team	Very intimate	Midwife or Doula

No matter the setting, your job's the same—be steady, be useful, and don't be the guy asking where to park during a contraction.

Logistics: Where to Go, When to Go, How Fast to Drive

It's not glamorous, but logistics matter. Don't wing it when things are already intense.

1. **Map it now, not later.** Do a dry run at night. Know where to park, which entrance to use, and whether you need to buzz in.

2. **Call first.** Some hospitals want you to call the nurse's line before showing up.

3. **Timing matters.** Don't wait for a dramatic water break. If contractions are regular—or she says, "I think it's time"—trust her. This isn't a test.

Hospital Birth (What We Did)

My wife was crystal clear: she wanted the epidural. She wanted the machines, the meds, the staff. Her take? If help's available, use it.

Hospitals bring structure—monitors, meds, and a small army of nurses and doctors. They also bring delays, shift changes, endless forms… and absolutely zero mood lighting.

- **Your role:** Be her translator and timekeeper. Nurses rotate. She's focused inward. You're the one who remembers when things started, what her preferences are, and where the extra snacks are hidden.

Home Birth (What My Brother Did)

My brother's wife gave birth at home, in their living room. It was intentional, intense, and deeply intimate. Midwife, doula, birth tub—it was beautiful, but demanding. No epidurals. No emergency button. You are the support crew.

- **Your role:** Set the tone and hold the line. That might mean pressing into her hips during contractions or restarting the playlist—again and again. You're not just "there"—you're actively involved.

Birth Center: The In-Between Zone

Birth centers have a cozy vibe—less clinical, more like a spa… except there's still a fetal monitor. They're run by midwives, usually near hospitals in case something shifts. But no overnight stays, so you're likely back home within hours.

- **Your role:** Create comfort. Light a candle if they allow it. Keep her hydrated. Be ready to carry everything back to the car when it's time to go home.

If your planned home or birth center delivery shifts to the hospital, your job is to pivot calm and fast. Keep the bag ready, the car gassed, and the mindset flexible.

💡 Dad Tip

Keep a line in your pocket: "Things changed, but I've got you. We're safe. We're okay."

☑ Arrival Checklist (So You Don't Look Lost)

Here's your must-pack list so you don't look lost when the action hits.

- ID, insurance card, hospital forms
- Birth plan—paper copy or phone screenshot
- Fully installed car seat and base—yes, the base too
- Bag for her: clothes, snacks, toiletries
- Bag for you: change of clothes, hoodie, toiletries
- Snacks and drinks—labor is long
- Phone charger with a long cable
- Pillow or blanket if she wants her own from home
- Folder for any paperwork or keepsakes

Stash an extra backup bag in the car—insurance if plans shift last minute. Even for home births, it's backup for the unexpected.

🎙 Real Talk

We had the car seat in the car, but hadn't installed the base. So there we were—baby in arms—watching how-to videos on our phones in the hospital parking lot. Shout-out to the nurse who stepped in and saved the day. Don't be me—install the thing before go-time.

> **☝ Mini Cheat Sheet for Dads**
> No time to overthink? Start here. This is your quick-hit list: what to remember, what to do, and what to say when it counts.
>
> - **Three things people forget:** your ID, extra socks, and a phone charger
> - **Two things to do if labor stalls:** walk together and offer quiet support—don't push fixes
> - **One line that always works:** "You're doing amazing. I've got you."

🧠 Dad Sanity Check
- Do I actually know where we're going and what's expected when we get there?
- Am I walking in prepared—or winging it and hoping for the best?
- Have I asked her what she needs from me in this setting?

💬 Reflection Prompt
What part of our birth plan feels locked in—and what's still fuzzy or unspoken? What can I clarify or prep this week to lower stress when it's go-time?

💡 Dad Tip: Know the setting—own the role.
It's hospital chaos, home birth calm, or something in between—you're the guy she's counting on. Not to have all the answers, but to keep things moving while she's doing the hardest work of her life.

So know where you're headed. Pack the bag. Buckle the car seat base. Be the guy who already thought of the next step—so she doesn't have to.

5.3: WHEN TO STEP IN, STEP BACK, OR STAY SILENT

This is the delivery-room dance. You're not the headliner, but you're absolutely on stage. Timing, presence, and restraint matter. You're reading the room, not running it.

Know Her Cues, Then Respect Them

Some partners want you right there—holding hands, breathing together, whispering encouragement. Others? They don't want anyone talking, touching, or even breathing too loud.

I learned fast that my "How are you doing?" every five minutes wasn't helping. I thought I was being attentive. She thought I was breaking her focus.

Read the room. Watch her face. Ask before labor, "What do you think you'll want from me when things get intense?" Then adjust.

Emergency Backup Tip

Plans shift. Stay grounded when things veer off course.

- If a C-section or curveball hits, stay calm. Ask, "What's the next step?"—then follow their lead.
- If the plan changes, don't freeze. Check in with her quietly and say, "Sound good to you?" Then adapt.

🗣 What Not to Say (Seriously, Don't)

We're wired to fix things, say stuff, offer encouragement. But this is not the time to drop a pep talk.

Here are some real-life "don't go there" phrases:

- "Just breathe." (Yeah, she knows. She's doing it.)
- "You're almost there!" (Unless you're a doctor staring at the baby's head... don't.)
- "This can't be worse than that time you ran a marathon." (Yes, a guy actually said that.)

My buddy once tried a dad joke. It bombed. He now calls it "The Look That Froze Time."

When to Step In

If she reaches for your hand? Take it.

If she's wincing and needs counter-pressure? You better be ready.

If she's dry-lipped and can't speak? Offer water or chapstick.

Small things are big things. I'll never forget how grateful my wife looked when I handed her a cool towel mid-contraction—just because I saw her sweating. She didn't say a word. But that eye contact said, "Thanks for showing up."

When to Step Back (Without Taking It Personally)
Some contractions come like freight trains. She might want silence, space, or to face a wall gripping the bed rail.

Don't hover. Don't sulk. Don't make it about you.

Step back. Sit. Stay alert.

💡 **Dad Tip**
If she faces a wall or pulls away, don't hover—sit or step back a few paces, but stay emotionally present.

When to Stay Silent
This is the hardest part for most of us—especially if you're used to being "the talker" in stress.

Silence can be strong. A quiet, steady presence feels safer than a guy narrating labor like it's a sports play-by-play.

If you don't know what to do? Just stay close. Eye contact, soft voice, and calm body language speak louder than words ever could.

> 🗣 **Script for Advocating Respectfully**
> You don't need to raise your voice to have her back. These lines help you speak up without escalating.
> - "She's not there yet. Can we ask a few questions first?"
> - "Can we slow down a sec? She's struggling right now."
> - "That's okay, but what other options do we have?"
>
> These lines show you've got her back—calm, clear, and protective.

💡 Dad Tip: Be Fully Present, Not Performative

This isn't your Best Supporting Actor moment. It's about showing up how she needs—not how you want to feel useful.

😳 Dad Sanity Check

- Am I actually helping—or just doing something to feel useful?
- Can I stay still, quiet, and calm if that's what she needs?
- Have I asked her what support looks like to her—not just what I assume?

💬 Reflection Prompt

When things get intense, what kind of support does she want—and what habits do I need to dial down so I don't miss the moment?

🎯 Quick Guide: Decision Flow (What to Do)

When things move fast, it helps to have a quick flow in your back pocket—something to glance at when your brain's fried and the room is spinning. Don't overthink—just scan and respond.

- Is she asking for something? Then respond. Water, counter-pressure, chapstick—just get it done.
- Is she breathing through a contraction? Stay quiet. Quiet support beats commentary every time.
- Is someone—staff or otherwise—being dismissive? Step in with a calm, supportive question.

In Action

These aren't big moves, but they hit big when she needs them. Be the guy who's ready without being asked.

- Keep your phone hidden—it beats scrolling memes during contractions.
- Bring a cold towel and chapstick—small things save the day.
- Your voice matters—pace your breathing with hers.
- Learn counter-pressure before the big day—practice on her lower back.

This moment is about being the anchor when the storm hits. Just show up and soak in the gravity of this together.

Later, you'll remember how quiet you were in those moments—and how much that presence meant.

5.4: SURVIVAL TIP #5—ADVOCATE WITHOUT OVERSTEPPING

Here's the deal: during labor, your partner might not be able to speak up—not because she doesn't want to, but because she's pushing a human out or bracing through contractions like a bus is rolling over her spine.

That's where you come in.

You're not the coach barking orders or the decision-maker calling audibles. You're the translator, the bodyguard, and the PR rep in one. Calm. Clear. Loyal. Locked in.

This is about knowing her wishes, watching the room, and stepping in when she can't—but without making it about you.

Know the Plan, Then Stay Flexible
Read the birth plan. I know, I know—it might look like a boring checklist. But it's really a cheat sheet to her hopes, fears, and "please don't let them do that unless they have to" items.

My wife had it dialed: "Yes" to the epidural, "No" to extra people in the room, "Maybe" to music—depending on her mood. And she made me read it while we were sitting in the hospital waiting for induction to start. Thank goodness she did, because everything changed real fast after that.

The monitors showed our daughter in distress. They tried everything—repositioning, oxygen, rolling her side to side—but nothing worked. Within minutes, they were wheeling her off for an emergency C-section, and I wasn't allowed in. It was terrifying. But because I knew the plan and had talked to her ahead of time, I didn't freeze. I could stay steady, ask the right questions, and show up afterward with what she needed.

Know the Plan, Know the Pivot
Birth doesn't follow a script. Things can change fast—fetal distress, stalled labor, sudden C-section. Your job? Don't freak. If you know her plan, you'll know how to roll with it. When things shift, lock eyes and ask, 'Are you good with this?' Then ride the wave with her. If the room's moving a million miles an hour, your calm is what she'll hold onto.

💡 **Dad Tip**
If things go sideways—emergency surgery, stalled labor, whatever—don't freeze. Breathe, stay close, and be the guy who doesn't panic. That's what she needs.

🗣 Speak Up, The Right Way
You don't need to know medical jargon. Your job is simple: listen, watch, and back her up with clear questions:

- "Can we take a minute before deciding?"
- "What are the risks of that option?"
- "Is there anything less invasive we can try first?"

This is about making sure her voice doesn't disappear in the chaos. Stay calm, stay steady, and they'll usually respect that.

Support Her Choices (Even If They Change)
You might go in thinking she wants to go unmedicated. But after a few hours of active labor, she says, "Give me the damn epidural." Your job isn't to question that call—it's to back her up and make sure she gets what she needs.

Maybe she wanted to avoid a C-section at all costs. But when the baby's heart rate dips, and the doctor says, "We need to move now," you make eye contact and say, "I've got you. Let's do what's safest."

Birth plans are guides, not contracts. The win is helping her feel seen, respected, safe—even when the game changes.

🎙 Real Talk: Our Emergency C-Section Story

Let me tell you how this played out for us.

My wife had to have an emergency C-section. Things escalated fast—one minute we were monitoring contractions, the next, they were wheeling her away. I followed close behind and was allowed into the OR once they got her prepped.

When I got in, they had already started the procedure, and I could see it in her face—she was struggling. I grabbed her hand, and she looked at me and said, "I don't feel right. I think I'm gonna puke." I flagged a nurse, fast. They handed me a barf bag, and there I was, holding it to her face as she vomited—while a team of doctors worked behind the curtain.

That was my moment to step in—nothing dramatic, nothing heroic. Just tuned in and ready to do whatever she needed.

She passed out after the baby was delivered—completely spent. So I went with the nurse to weigh our daughter. Just me and this tiny human I'd just met. After that, I carried her to the recovery room and held her while we waited for her mom to wake up.

It was scary. It was surreal. And it was unforgettable.

If You're Separated During Birth

This happened to me during our emergency C-section—and I want you to hear it now, so if it happens to you, you don't feel lost, useless, or like you're out of the fight.

Sometimes you're not allowed in—certain surgeries, policy changes, whatever. It sucks. But you're still in it.

- Ask a nurse: "How can I support her from out here?"
- Keep checking in—updates matter.
- Breathe slow. Write down anything you want to say or ask later.
- When they bring the baby out, your calm presence is the first safe thing that tiny human sees. That's your job. Own it.

💡 Dad Tip: Know the Mission—Then Watch the Room

Real advocacy is quiet, steady, dialed in. Stay present. Stay available. And when it's time to speak up, speak with clarity and care.

🐣 Dad Sanity Check

- What's one part of her birth preferences I haven't asked her about yet?
- Do I know what her biggest fears are around labor?
- Am I ready to speak for her—not over her—if it comes to that?

💬 Reflection Prompt

- Do I know what she wants—and what she might need if things change?
- How can I be ready to speak up for her, without speaking over her?

🎯 Bonus Move: The Birth Plan Snapshot

Take a pic of the birth plan and save it in your Notes app or on your lock screen. That way you've got it—even if the paper copy gets buried under hospital forms and blankets.

Want it ready-made? The printable Birth Plan Snapshot is in the Book Bonuses (QR code in the intro).

Wrap-Up: You did it. You stayed in it when things got wild.
You showed up when she needed you most.

You weren't running the show—but you made sure her voice was heard, even when she couldn't find the words.

Maybe it didn't go how you pictured it. That's okay. You didn't flinch. You stayed steady. And now you're holding proof that it mattered.

Deep breath. The real work's next—but you've already proven you're built for it.

📋 BIRTH PLAN SNAPSHOT (DAD'S CHEAT SHEET)

🦉 Basics
- Mom's Name: _____
- Baby's Name (if chosen): _____
- OB/Midwife Contact Info: _____
- Birth Location: _____

📞 Emergency Contacts
- Partner: _____ | ▦ _____
- Backup Support Person: _____ | ▦ _____
- Pediatrician (if known): _____ | ▦ _____

🖊 Pain Management
- Epidural ASAP
- Open to epidural—see how it goes
- Unmedicated as long as possible
- Gas & Air / Nitrous Oxide
- Walking epidural
- Comfort-focused first (breathing, movement, etc.)

🕯 Environment Preferences
- Dim lights
- Music playlist (name: _____)
- Low room traffic
- Familiar items from home (blanket, pillow)

👤 Support People
- Partner
- Doula
- Specific family/friend (who: _____)
- No additional people unless cleared

⚠ Interventions & Decisions
- Okay to induce if needed
- Prefer to avoid unless medically necessary
- Open to membrane sweep
- Okay with breaking water if needed
- Want to ask questions before any changes

☠ C-Section Preferences
- Partner in OR
- Delayed cord clamping
- Clear drape / early contact if possible
- Partner stays with baby if separated

👶 After Delivery
- Skin-to-skin ASAP
- Delay first bath
- Feeding plan: Breast / Formula / Combo
- Baby stays with us unless medically necessary
- Partner goes with baby if mom can't

🛡 Special Notes
- Know the plan—but stay flexible
- If labor changes fast, keep her calm and informed
- Speak up calmly: "Can we ask a few questions?"
- You're her advocate, not her decision-maker

💬 Quick Dad Reminders
- She's in charge—you're her voice, not her boss
- Don't argue—ask, confirm, stay steady
- Be the calm presence. Breathe. Repeat.

PART 6

THE FOURTH TRIMESTER—LIFE WITH A NEWBORN

"Babies are always more trouble than you thought—and more wonderful."
—Charles Osgood

The baby's here—and it's a full-on blur.

You're running on no sleep. She's recovering from the most physical thing she's ever done. And this little human? Crying, feeding, pooping like clockwork. You're not sure what time it is. Or the last time you ate. Or if that noise was the baby, your dog, or your own stomach.

This phase hits like a storm. And no one hands you a manual—or a break. I thought I was ready. But nothing prepares you for how fast the shift happens. One day you're packing a hospital bag. Next day, you're frantically searching online for "is green poop normal" while trying to find clean burp cloths and remember your Wi-Fi password.

This section is your lifeline. No fluff. Just the basics you need to keep the wheels on—diapers, bottles, feeding, sleep (what little you get), and staying connected with your partner while everything's upside down.

You don't have to be perfect. You do have to be present. Let's get you through the fog with your sanity (mostly) intact.

6.1: DIAPERS, BOTTLES—AND WTF JUST HAPPENED?

You've heard it before, but there's no real prep for this. One minute you're cheering in the delivery room; the next, you're staring at a diaper blowout that somehow went everywhere. Welcome to the first days: no sleep, no guide, just nonstop tiny chaos.

The Glitch Is Real

There's no rhythm. You're stumbling through 3 a.m. feedings and diaper changes like a glitching NPC—basically a video game character stuck on repeat—and that's okay. Nobody's expecting a dad to nail this, especially not right away.

I once changed a diaper mid-step... while holding a screaming baby. It felt like a weird balancing act, and then—boom—you realize you're doing it.

Fake it 'til you don't need to.

But here's the part nobody really warns you about: those first couple of days are a straight-up WTF marathon. Everything feels off the rails—and most of it is totally normal.

WTF: The First 48 Hours

Nobody warns you about this stuff—but it's all part of the ride. Here's what's weird, messy, and completely normal:

- **Meconium:** Your baby's first poop looks like tar. Thick, black, sticky tar. It'll freak you out—but it's exactly what's supposed to happen. Two days later, it's gone and you're on to mustard-colored blowouts.
- **Weird bellybutton stump:** It'll look gnarly before it falls off. Dry, scabby, sometimes with a little crust. Don't pick at it. It'll drop off on its own in a couple weeks.
- **Cluster feeding:** Baby may want to feed constantly—sometimes every 45 minutes. It feels like you just finished one feed when the next starts. It's exhausting—but totally normal and often a sign they're boosting supply.

- Crying spells: Some babies cry for hours, no matter what you do. It doesn't mean you're failing. Sometimes they just need to cry while you hold steady.
- Post-birth recovery zone: Your partner just did the most physical thing imaginable. There will be bleeding, pads, mesh underwear, soreness, and swelling. Respect that zone. Get her water, snacks, meds, or a pillow—don't just hover and ask if she's "okay."

Diaper Life 101

Yep, You're the Guy Now. Welcome to the front lines. Newborns pee and poop like it's their job. And it kind of is. You're looking at 8–12 diaper changes a day, and yes, sometimes back-to-back. Here's what helps:

- **The blue line trick:** Most diapers have a little line that turns blue if there's pee. Poop won't always trigger it—your nose will.
- **Wipe under the butt** before pulling the diaper off—it catches sneak attacks.
- **If it's a boy, always point the penis down.** Rookie mistake otherwise. You might want a pee-pee teepee or just a cloth to cover him mid-change. That arc is real.
- **Wipe front to back**—always. Especially important for baby girls to prevent infections.
- **One hand always on the baby.** No exceptions. They roll like tiny ninjas.
- **Create a change zone.** Keep everything in reach: diapers, wipes, clean clothes, trash bin. It's not glamorous, but it's your battlefield.

Once, I changed my daughter's blowout thinking we were in the clear—then she launched a follow-up round that nailed me square in the chest. I looked down, and there it was: a perfect, heart-shaped poo splat on my shirt. Romantic, right? From that day on, I learned—contain the scene. Bathroom changes only for code brown. Clean the baby and your dignity with a solid bath.

Feeding Frontlines

Feeding a newborn is one of the most physically and emotionally demanding parts of the early days—for both of you. Here's what matters most, and where you can actually make a difference.

Breastfeeding isn't always automatic.

Latching might be tough. Milk might be slow to come in. She might be in pain. That's not failure—it's super common. Ask for a lactation consultant early— they're used to the tears and stress and they want to help.

Here's what you can do:

- **Hydration station:** Keep a full water bottle next to her—always. Dehydration is a supply killer.
- **Hot compresses:** For clogged ducts or pain, a warm compress or heated rice sock can help.
- **Snack patrol:** Oats, protein, healthy fats—she needs fuel. Keep the snacks flowing while she's stuck under a nursing pillow.
- **Moral support:** If she's crying mid-feed or frustrated with the latch, hold the baby, hold her hand, hold the line. No fixing—just presence.

Low supply?

Sometimes it's just rest, water, and food. Sometimes it's hormones or stress. It's not her fault—and it's not yours to fix. Don't push. Don't panic. Ask what she needs, listen hard, and back it.

If things feel stuck, suggest calling in backup: a lactation consultant, midwife, or someone who knows the ropes. Getting help early can change everything.

If you're bottle-feeding (or combo-feeding):

If you're bottle-feeding or doing both, here's the stuff that saves time, sanity, and shirt changes.

- Sanitize every part: Before first use and after each feed. You can boil, use a sterilizer, or a dishwasher basket. Keep it consistent.

- Test bottle types: Start with a common one, like Dr. Brown's, Comotomo, or whatever the hospital gives you. Don't buy a dozen of anything. Some babies are picky about nipple flow, shape, or feel.
- Warm milk just right: A bottle warmer or warm water cup works. Test it on your wrist—should feel like nothing (body temp).
- Don't force it: Some feeds will take forever. Some will get rejected. Stay cool and try again in 10 minutes.

🎙 Real Talk
Our daughter rejected every bottle—except one random freebie from a hospital kit. We ran out at 3 a.m. and ended up overnighting it off Amazon. Lesson: follow the baby's lead, not the box branding.

Watch for feeding cues:
Feeding cues can be subtle—until they're not. Spot them early, and you'll save everyone a meltdown.

- Rooting (turning toward a touch)
- Lip smacking or tongue flicking
- Fussing or hands to mouth
- Crying: If you're here, you've missed the cues. That's overtime—you're playing catch-up.

Night Shift Game Plan (Sample Division of Labor)
Sleep's a luxury. A game plan makes it slightly less chaotic—and keeps you both from silently resenting each other at 4 a.m. When you're both running on fumes, having a default system helps:

- You do the **diaper change** first—quiet, quick, low light.
- She does the **feeding** (if breastfeeding).
- You handle the **burp and settle** the baby back down.
- Then you both try to pass out until the next round.

Tag in, tag out. Teamwork isn't optional. It's survival.

💡 Dad Tip: Focus on the Role, Not Perfection

You won't nail everything. Good. That's not the point. Show up. Stay in it. That's what matters.

- Rotate chores: One day you do the feeding. The next, you handle diaper duty.
- Keep a stash: Wipes, diapers, burp cloths, and snacks within arm's reach—stock that bedside caddy.
- **Label bottles:** Use tiny sticky notes at first so you know who's feeding when.
- Learn soothing techniques: Try swaddling, shushing, swinging, and skin-to-skin. Watch what works—you'll get it.

"Wait, Is That Normal?" (Newborn Edition)

Newborns are weird. If you're looking up "is it normal if…" every five minutes, this list's for you. Don't panic if:

- Baby's poop turns green or mustard-seedy—totally normal.
- They feed every hour… then sleep five straight.
- They sneeze, hiccup, or grunt like a tiny old man.
- Their skin flakes or looks blotchy at first.
- They cry like they're auditioning for a horror movie—sometimes for reasons you'll never figure out.

🧠 Dad Sanity Check

- What am I pretending to understand when I don't? (Techniques, timing, trust your partner more than your instincts here.)
- Have I asked my partner or a nurse one question today—anything?

💬 Reflection Prompt

What's one part of newborn care I've been avoiding—and how can I lean into it without overthinking it?

In Action

This is how you learn—by doing the reps. Try what makes sense, toss what doesn't, and keep showing up.

- **Diaper reps:** Do every single diaper change for 24 hours. Learn that blue line and how it feels to reset a blowout.
- **Bottle test:** Try two or three different nipples. Track what worked—ditch what didn't.
- **Cry-responder:** Pick one soothing trick (like swaddle or walk) and stick with it until you know it works for your kid.
- **Talk it out:** Narrate what you're doing—even if it's just to calm your own nerves: "Here we go. Fresh diaper…"

Why This Matters

You won't remember every diaper or bottle. But you'll remember those quiet 3 a.m. moments when it felt like everything was falling apart—and you stayed. That's what sticks. For her. For your baby. For you.

6.2: SURVIVAL TIP #6—SURVIVAL BASICS, NOT MASTERY

Your job isn't to be a baby whisperer—it's to show up.

Forget mastering parenting right now. This is survival mode, my dude—diapers, bottles, burping, soothing. That's your squad. Learn just enough to get through the day (and night) without burning out. The rest? You'll learn by doing, and by screwing up a little. That's part of the game.

Baby Cry Decoder – What That Wail Might Actually Mean

Baby cries don't come with subtitles. But after a while, you'll start noticing patterns. Different cries can mean different things—sometimes.

Let's break down the most common types of cries you're likely to hear in the first few months, and what they might mean. Keyword: might. You're not psychic. You're just trying to survive and help a tiny person who doesn't have words yet.

- **The Hunger Cry:** It usually starts low and rhythmic, like a steady "wah, wah, wah," that builds if you ignore it.It might be paired with rooting—like turning their head and sucking on whatever's nearby (shirt, blanket, your thumb).

  What to do: Offer a bottle or help your partner nurse. Don't wait until it escalates. If you're not sure they're hungry? Offer anyway. Hunger is the boss level of baby needs.

- **The Gassy or Grunty Cry:** This one sounds strained—like your baby's working hard in there. You might hear grunting, fussing, or general discomfort noises, especially after feeding or during diaper time. Legs might pull up or they'll arch their back.

  What to do: Try burping, bicycling their legs, or giving a gentle tummy massage. Sometimes they just need help letting it out (literally).

- The Sleepy Cry: This one can be whiny, nasal, and a little breathy—like your baby is too tired to even cry properly. They might rub their eyes or look zoned out before the meltdown starts.

  What to do: Swaddle, rock, dim the lights. Get them into a calm space with less stimulation. Don't try to play your way out of it. They're telling you they're done.

- The "I Hate Everything" Cry: Sharp, sudden cries—like your baby is yelling at the universe. It's often overstimulation or just a general meltdown: too much noise, too much light, too much of everything.

  What to do: Take them somewhere quiet. Hold them close. Talk in a soft, steady voice. Sometimes the world's just too much, and they need a reset.

- The Random Cry: This is the cry that makes no sense. They're fed, clean, burped, held, and still losing it. This is where your patience gets tested.

  What to do: Try a change of scenery—walk around, wear them in a carrier, bounce on a yoga ball, hum, whatever. Some babies just need to vent. Be their safe place to do it.

Your job is to respond calmly. You're learning your baby's "settings" one cry at a time. Some cries blend together. Some mean nothing at all. And some nights, they just cry because it's 2 a.m. and they're babies.

♀ Dad Tip

If your baby's inconsolable for hours or you're seeing weird spit-up, call the doc. Could be reflux or colic—both are real and brutal.

Burping Basics (AKA The Gas Boss)

If your baby's squirming mid-feed or acting possessed, gas is the usual suspect. Here's what actually works:

- **Over the shoulder:** Hold baby upright and pat or rub gently—firm enough to help, not like you're playing bongos.
- **Sitting upright:** Support the head, lean them slightly forward on your palm, and pat or rub the back.
- **Lying across your lap:** Place baby tummy-down, legs hanging, and pat or rub the back. Works well mid-nap if they start squirming.
- **Take breaks to burp:** Don't wait until they're done chugging. Burp them mid-feed if needed.

♀ Dad Tip

Keep a burp cloth locked and loaded— your shoulder will take the hit.

Cry Decoder Quick Reference
Need a fast refresher at 2 a.m.? Here's a cheat sheet to help you figure out what the wailing might mean—and what to try first.

Cry Type	What It Sounds Like	What It Might Mean	What to Try
Hunger Cry	Rhythmic, low-pitched, gets louder	Baby's hungry	Offer a feeding (bottle or breast)
Gassy Cry	Grunty, strained, fussy	Tummy trouble or trapped gas	Burp, bicycle legs, gentle tummy rub
Sleepy Cry	Whiny, breathy, weak-sounding	Overtired, overstimulated	Swaddle, rock, reduce light/sound
Overstimulated Cry	Sharp, loud, frustrated	Too much going on	Move to quiet space, hold them close
Random Cry	Inconsistent, nothing seems to help	Just having a moment	Walk, hold, change scenery, stay calm

Soothing Like a Pro (Even If You're Clueless)

You'll hear about 'The 5 S's' from Harvey Karp's "Happiest Baby on the Block." They actually help. When nothing else works, these moves buy everyone peace (and maybe sleep):

- **Swaddle:** A straightjacket of comfort. Use Velcro ones if you hate origami.
- **Side or stomach position (for holding, not sleeping):** Cradle them on their side or stomach along your arm—helps with gas.
- **Shush:** Don't whisper—go loud. Think white noise machine in your mouth.
- **Swing:** Gentle bouncing or rocking—rhythm helps reset their little nervous systems.
- **Suck:** A pacifier can be magic. Or your pinky if you're desperate.

Baby Wearing Equals Instant Calm Down

Some newborns hate being put down. Our first kid had a sixth sense—tiptoe away, boom, wide awake and screaming. If your baby acts like a heat-seeking missile, baby wearing might save you—instant calm, hands-free style:

🎙 **Real Talk**

I rocked the Baby K'tan—no buckles, no ninja wrapping, just loop it over and go. My wife preferred structured carriers like the Ergo for longer walks or outdoor stuff.

Baby Carrier Breakdown

Not all carriers are created equal—and trying them cold during a scream fest isn't ideal.

Here's the quick lowdown:

Cloth Wraps (Moby, Baby K'tan)

- Cozy for newborns
- K'tan is easy, pre-sized
- Con: Can be hot or awkward for bigger babies

Structured Buckle Carriers (Ergo, BabyBjörn)

- Great support, adjustable
- Best for longer wear or bigger babies
- Con: Bulky, takes a sec to strap in

Hybrids (Lillebaby, Boba X)

- Best of both worlds
- Con: Higher price point, slight learning curve

💡 **Dad Tip**

Practice baby-wearing before meltdown hour—you'll look less like you're wrestling a cloth burrito.

3 Things You Can Learn This Week That Actually Help
These aren't deep-dive parenting hacks—just quick wins that make your life easier and your baby calmer. Try 'em this week, and you'll feel way less lost:

- **Burping moves** (try all three—lap, shoulder, seated)
- **Your baby's "I'm hungry" cue** (usually before the full meltdown)
- **How to swaddle like a boss** (or which wrap she actually tolerates)

Dad MVP Moves: Quick Wins That Actually Help
You want to show up without overthinking it? Here's a cheat sheet. Do these regularly, and you're already crushing it:

- Refill her water without being asked
- Take the 3 a.m. shift so she can sleep
- Run a solo diaper mission—no "Hey Babe, where are the wipes?" interruptions.
- Prep snacks she actually likes and stash them where she feeds
- Say "You're doing amazing"—and mean it

These don't require perfect timing. Repeat them enough and you'll be the default legend she brags about in her mom group.

💬 **Reflection Prompt**
Which MVP move surprised you by helping your partner—or you—most this week?

💡 **Dad Tip: Learn by Doing, Not Watching**
You don't have to be good—you just have to get in there. Every diaper, bottle, and burp builds your confidence and connection.

🧠 **Dad Sanity Check**
What's one thing I've been avoiding because I'm afraid of messing up?

Swaddling? Bottle making? Bath time? Pick one, screw it up—get better.

That's how this works.

6.3: NEWBORN SLEEP (OR LACK THEREOF)

First truth bomb: newborns don't "sleep through the night." That myth was either invented by baby book writers—or parents with unicorn babies. Here's reality: sleep comes in short, random bursts—2 to 3 hours tops, if you're lucky. That doesn't mean nighttime sleep is broken down. It means it was never intact. Day, night, morning—they don't care. They're on the infant loop: eat, explode, pass out, repeat. Brutal—but livable. Newborns don't care about your circadian rhythm. They're on an infant loop: eat, poop, scream, pass out, repeat. Brutal—but survivable. You just need to adjust expectations and protect sleep like it's your Wi-Fi password on fantasy draft night.

Welcome to the Sleep Blender
The first couple weeks feel like a casino: no windows, no clocks, too many lights at the wrong times. Days blur into nights. You start wondering if 3 a.m. is technically "morning" or "late last night."

Sleep deprivation hits harder when there's no end in sight. You'll say weird stuff. You'll cry at random. You might even forget your own zip code. Your partner? Probably in the same boat—except she's also healing from childbirth and possibly breastfeeding around the clock.

Sleep won't "get better" overnight. But it does get more manageable if you treat it like a shared resource, not a competition.

Newborn Sleep Snapshot (What's Actually Normal)
Here's your sleep stat cheat sheet—what's normal, what's chaos, and why it doesn't mean you're screwing it up.

Sleep Stat	What to Expect
Total Sleep	Many newborns sleep 16–18 hours in 3–4 hours bursts
Wake Windows	Every 2–3 hours (yes, even overnight)
Day/Night Confusion	100%—they don't know night from day yet

Sleep Trades: Your New Favorite Move

You and your partner don't have to be awake at the same time unless something's on fire. Here's the move:

- **Split shifts:** One of you handles the early part of the night (say, 9 p.m. to 2 a.m.), the other handles the back half (2 a.m. to 7 a.m.).
- **Tag naps:** When the baby naps, decide who's "on" and who can crash. Yes, naps count.
- **Use the bottle:** If your partner is breastfeeding, once pumping is established, take one of the night feeds off her plate. If you're formula feeding—tag in, bro. No excuses.

💡 **Dad Tip**

A 3-hour nap feels like a vacation when you haven't slept in a week. Don't underestimate the power of a tiny recharge.

Who's On Duty: Easy Rotation Ideas

You don't need a military-grade schedule—but a loose system keeps both of you from losing it. Here are a few easy handoff strategies that won't fry your brain.

- Tag-team naps: One of you naps while the other is "on call."
- Night block handoff: Trade off every 4–5 hours.
- Weekday/weekend swaps: One sleeps in one day, the other the next.
- Use a whiteboard or sticky note to track shifts—sleep brain makes it easy to forget.

Dad Myths That Need Busting

Let's kill off a few lies that keep dads stuck in the sidelines—or thinking they get a weekend pass.

- "I'll just help more on weekends."
  Nope. Babies don't care what day it is—she needs support every day.
- "If she's breastfeeding, I can't do anything."

Wrong. You can burp, diaper, swaddle, soothe, prep snacks, clean pump parts—and be the calm in the chaos.

The Silent Killers: Sleep Envy & Resentment
It creeps in quietly—you see her sleeping peacefully while you're rocking a screaming baby, and suddenly you're keeping score.

Don't.

This isn't a competition—it's a survival team. If you're feeling resentment build, it's usually a sign that you haven't had a break in too long. Speak up. Not to blame—just to plan. Say: "Hey, I'm fried. Can we figure out a better system?" It's not just the baby running on fumes—you are too. Here's how sleep deprivation shows up for us as dads.

What Running on Fumes Actually Looks Like
You probably won't say "I'm overwhelmed"—most guys don't. But the signs sneak up. If any of this sounds familiar, it's not because you suck at this. It's just sleep brain doing its thing.

- We snap at stuff that normally wouldn't bug us
- We zone out mid-convo and forget what we were doing
- We crave alone time but feel guilty taking it
- We obsess over tiny tasks instead of resting
- We feel numb, like we're just clocking in and out

You're not failing. You're fried. Step out, catch your breath, grab 20 minutes. That's how you stay in the game—not bail on it.

💡 **Dad Tip: Sleep-Deprived Does not Equal Emotionally Broken**
If you're feeling ragey, fragile, or hollow—it's not because you're failing. It's because you're running at 4% battery while carrying the whole house. Sleep loss distorts everything. Don't trust the 3 a.m. voice that says you're doing it wrong. Trust what rested you knows.

Set the Sleep Scene (For Baby, and You)

You can't force a newborn to sleep—but you *can* give them (and you) a better shot. Think of this like dimming the lights before a movie. It's not magic—but it helps.

- **Keep it dark:** Use blackout curtains and avoid overhead lights at night.
- **White noise:** It helps drown out every creak and sigh that otherwise sends you into panic mode.
- **Consistent signals:** Swaddle, feed, dark room, soft noise—sleep cue. Your baby won't always respond, but it helps set a rhythm.

Now let's talk about where your baby sleeps—because that decision's going to affect how much sleep you get too.

Sleep Logistics: Where the Baby Sleeps (And What That Means for You)

- **Bassinet vs. Crib:** In the early days, a bassinet next to your bed is the move. You'll be up every couple of hours anyway, and it's easier to reach over than walk across the room or down the hall. Save the crib for longer stretches—or naps if you need the space.
- **Co-sleeping:** It's real. Some parents swear by it, others steer clear. The American Academy of Pediatrics recommends **room-sharing without bed-sharing** for at least the first six months. Ideally the first year, to reduce the risk of SIDS. That means baby in a bassinet or crib nearby, not in your bed. But if you're considering bed-sharing out of desperation, at least do it informed: firm mattress, no loose bedding, no pillows near the baby. No shame—just be safe.

Should you nap when the baby naps? Yeah, if you can. But let's be real: sometimes that's when the laundry happens, or the dishes, or a sandwich. Try to trade off with your partner. If the baby naps and one of you can rest—even for 20 minutes—it helps. A lot.

⚲ Dad Tip: Protect Sleep Like It's Oxygen

Yours. Hers. The baby's. Sleep isn't a luxury—it's fuel. Without it, you're cranky, clumsy, and likely to cry while microwaving oatmeal (ask me how I know). Guard your sleep like you guard the remote during the playoffs.

⊛ Dad Sanity Check

What's keeping me from sleeping—and what can I change?

- Am I doomscrolling instead of resting?
- Am I refusing help because I think I have to "tough it out"?
- Have I actually communicated what I need—or just assumed it's hopeless?

You're not weak for needing sleep. You're human.

♡ Reflection Prompt

What's one thing I can do this week to protect sleep—for me, for her, or for both of us—without waiting for permission?

6.4: STAYING CONNECTED TO YOUR PARTNER (EVEN ON 2 HOURS OF SLEEP)

Nobody warns you how weird it feels to stay close when you're both running on fumes and everything smells faintly of sour milk.

Those first few weeks? It's like co-managing a tiny crisis center—only the crisis is cute, screaming, and covered in spit-up. Conversations shift from "I love you" to "Did we order more wipes?" in record time. You're exhausted. She's touched-out. And romance? It's probably buried somewhere under the laundry pile.

It's normal—but it's a quiet trap. Survival mode can turn into default mode, and connection doesn't survive on autopilot.

You're on different planets emotionally, maybe even physically. But you're still in this together—and that's where the work begins.

Name the Drift Before It Becomes a Canyon

You might feel like something's off. Not broken. Not bad. Just... distant.

That shift happens when your conversations become all logistics—diapers, feeds, burp cloth counts—and none of the deeper stuff. That doesn't mean your relationship is failing. It just means **you're both in the thick of it.**

But here's the truth: disconnection doesn't usually announce itself with a bang. It sneaks in. You drift. You start living next to each other instead of with each other.

And reconnecting? It doesn't require a grand gesture or a weekend away. It just takes **small moves, done often.**

💡 Dad Tip: A 2-Minute Check-In Beats Hours of Silence

Just ask, "How are you feeling?" or "What do you need from me right now?"

Real-Life Disconnects

Sometimes, the disconnection isn't loud. It's the silence. The missed eye contact. The fact that neither of you has used the word "we" in a few days. You're both running on fumes, and it's easy to slip into parallel play—doing life side by side, but not together.

Little rifts show up like:

1. She's feeling touched out, and you're feeling shut out.
2. You think you're being helpful, and she thinks you're hovering.
3. You both start assuming instead of asking.

Call it out early—not in a dramatic way. Just "Hey, I feel like we're off. Can we figure out five minutes to just breathe and check in?"

Keep the Romance Real

Forget candlelit dinners for now—the love that matters is low-key, show-up-without-being-asked kind.

That means:

- Giving her a break when she doesn't ask for one.
- Noticing she needs water or a snack before she does.
- Saying "thank you" for the fifth diaper change of the day.

It's not flashy. But it's what holds you together.

☉ Mini Moves That Matter

This isn't about doing more. These are quick hits that actually land—especially when you're both fried.

- Text her from the next room: "You good?"
- Make her coffee how she likes it. Bring it to her before she even asks.
- Rub her back—no strings attached.
- Tell her one thing you're proud of her for—something specific.
- Let her nap. Don't just offer—make it happen.

🗣 Quick Check-Ins

If you're away at work or just in the other room, shoot a one-liner:

- "Are you holding up okay?"
- "Do you need anything before I come back in?"
- "Want to trade places for a bit?"

It doesn't have to be long. Just a blip of care. A well-timed check-in can reroute a whole crappy day.

Tag-In Touch
Physical connection can feel off right now—she might be sore, touched out, or just not in the headspace for more than survival. That doesn't mean touch disappears. It just evolves.

Try this:

- Hand on her back while she's feeding the baby.
- Kiss her forehead while passing the baby.
- Sit close enough to let your legs touch while watching TV.

It says "I'm here" without a word.

Remind Her: She's Still Your Person
In the baby haze, it's easy to only see "mom" and "dad" and forget the rest. But she's still your person. Your partner. The one you fell in love with before the burp cloths and night feeds.

Say it. Show it. Even if your love language right now is just delivering a hot meal and a moment of quiet.

🗨 Conversation Starters That Don't Feel Forced
You don't need to turn into a poet. But if you want to stay emotionally close, try these on a walk, before bed, or during a random baby nap:

- "What's one thing that felt good today?"
- "What's been secretly annoying you?"
- "Is there something I can take off your plate this week?"
- "When did you feel most like yourself this week?"

They open the door without requiring either of you to bust out a therapy session. No pressure, just space.

♀ Dad Tip

Stick one on the mirror, the coffee maker, or the pump station. Timing beats poetry.

When You're Tapped Out Too

Being the steady one doesn't mean you don't get drained. You can still support her and refill your own tank. Try:

- Step outside for 5 deep breaths
- Text a friend: "Today = rough"
- Ask: "Can we tag out for 30 mins?"

Quick Connection Moves for Tired Dads

No time? No energy? No problem. These low-effort moves still count—big time.

- Text from the next room: "Need anything?"
- Bring water, snacks, or coffee before she asks
- Offer her a nap—and make it happen
- Leave a Post-it with: "Still your person."
- Sit close and let your knees touch—no words needed

If You're the One Feeling Disconnected

It's not just her. You might feel lonely too—like you've been replaced by a diaper genie and a feeding chart. Try one of these small resets:

- Send her a text that says: "I miss us—not just the team, but the you-and-me part."
- Plan a tiny 10-minute hangout—coffee, couch, no baby talk.
- Say what you need: "I could really use a hug today."

Connection is a two-way street—even when the road's covered in burp cloths.

💡 Dad Tip Recap: Staying Connected on Low Battery

- Check in—even a two-minute convo beats the weird silence
- Say "I miss us" out loud—not just in your head
- Offer touch with zero expectations
- Drop a one-liner that cuts through the noise
- Protect both alone time and connection time

This isn't about doing more. It's about staying human, even when you're running on crumbs.

🧠 Dad Sanity Check

What do I need more of—connection, alone time, or just permission to admit I'm tapped out?

Be honest. Then talk about it. No blame, just truth. That kind of honesty builds connection more than any grand gesture ever could.

💬 Reflection Prompt

What's one small thing I can do this week to feel more connected—to her, to myself, or both?

6.5: SUPPORTING RECOVERY WHILE MANAGING CHAOS

Here's the part nobody tells you: Delivery's the starting line, not the finish. She just ran a marathon and got hit by a truck—at the same time. Now she's expected to be functional, emotional, maternal—while leaking from multiple places and running on zero sleep.

Your job now? Buffer. Fixer. Quiet MVP.
This phase is messy, loud, and unpredictable—but that's why your role matters even more. Not to fix everything. Not to micromanage. But to quietly handle the chaos **so she doesn't have to.**

Small Wins Matter More Than Big Gestures
Forget flowers or "push presents" (yeah, that's the fancy gift some people give moms after birth). Real support looks like this:

- Folded laundry that just… appeared.
- A sandwich you handed her while she nursed.
- A fresh water bottle placed beside her before she even asked.

No one's clapping—but you're stacking trust and recovery points that matter more than words right now.

Top 5 Things She Shouldn't Have to Ask For
Want to be her MVP? Handle the stuff she shouldn't have to spell out. These basics say more than a thousand "Can you…?"

- Meals that show up—no planning, no prep needed
- Laundry that just gets done
- Someone to hold the baby so she can shower in peace
- A real "You're doing enough"—and mean it when you say it
- A quiet reminder to take her meds or sip some water

⚙ **Mini Moves That Matter**

Not sure what she needs? Start here—you'll rarely go wrong.

- **Pre-load her water bottle.** Hydration without asking.
- **Put snacks within reach.** Nursing and recovery burn calories. Trail mix or granola bars go a long way.
- **Run interference with visitors:** "Let's check in before we schedule anything."
- **Tidy one room a day.** Clean spaces = calm minds.
- **Start the laundry, fold it later.** Progress counts.
- **Tell her one thing she's doing well.** Mean it. Keep it simple.
- **Hold the baby without needing a handoff.** Just let her rest.

Recovery Mode: What She'll Need From You—For Real

We talked about this back in Section 5.1, but now you're living it. She's healing, the baby's screaming, and you're the glue holding the operation together. What she needs from you depends on how delivery went—but in both cases, your job is hands-on, observant, and steady.

- **If she had a vaginal birth:** Expect soreness, swelling, maybe stitches or tearing. Even going to the bathroom might hurt. Emotionally, it can be a rollercoaster.

  Your move: Stock the bathroom with a peri bottle, pads, and cooling spray. Take care of meals, dishes, and diapers so she can sit, bleed, breathe, and recover without being in motion 24/7.

- **If she had a C-section:** This isn't "just another birth"—it's major abdominal surgery. She's dealing with pain, mobility issues, meds, and full-body exhaustion.

Your move: Help her sit up and move slowly. Be the one lifting the baby. Manage her meds—track the timing, hand them to her, set reminders. Keep an eye on the incision site (redness, discharge, fever means call someone). Don't downplay it—this is real recovery, not just soreness.

Support C-Section Recovery Like a Champ

A C-section is major surgery—and she shouldn't have to script your next move. Even if she's acting fine, she's healing from something huge. She might need help getting up, reaching for the baby, or even laughing without it hurting. Don't make her ask. Step in early and often:

- Manage the meds—track timing, hand them to her, set reminders
- Be the baby runner—diapers, feeds, burps
- Handle meals, pillows, the remote—everything
- Protect her rest like it's sacred

🎙 **Real Talk**

My wife had a C-section both times. And honestly? I didn't know how to help at first. She's super independent—doesn't like asking for help—and I didn't want to overstep. But I figured out fast: if I waited for instructions, I missed the moment.

So I just started doing things. I brought the baby over for feeds. I handled every diaper. I made sure she had snacks and meds and could sleep without stressing. The more I stepped in, the better she felt, the more confident I got.

Support isn't hero moves—it's seeing what needs to happen and doing it before she asks.

💡 **Dad Tip: Adjust Your Gameplan Daily**

Don't assume she's "back to normal" just because she stood up or smiled. Healing isn't linear. Stay flexible. Ask how she's doing, but also look at how she's doing. That'll tell you more.

Low-Effort Tracking Equals Fewer Drop Balls

You're both running on fumes, and stuff will get forgotten. Here's how to keep small tasks from slipping through the cracks:

- Sticky notes on the fridge (old school, still works)

- Whiteboard by the changing station
- Shared app (Google Keep, Todoist, Calendar) so tasks stick

If it's on the board, it's real. No more "I thought you did it" fights.

Lock Down the Logistics
You don't need to be a chef or a housekeeper. Just do what needs doing.

1. **Keep the fridge stocked.** Groceries equal peace of mind.
2. **Dishes done and diapers restocked.** No one notices when they're handled—but everyone notices when they're not.
3. **Visitors? Gatekeep hard.** "Now's not a good time" is a complete sentence. If she wants space, you enforce it. If she wants her mom there, fine—but you set the tone.

💡 **Dad Tip**
Act like the guest room's closed for renovations. No one else gets access unless she says so.

Advocate. Anticipate. Don't Ask for a Medal.
There's a fine line between supporting and hovering. Don't make her manage your helpfulness. Try this:

- **Anticipate needs.** Trash full? Take it out. Baby crying? See if you can soothe first.
- **Speak up for her.** If a nurse, visitor, or family member is pushing too hard, step in kindly but clearly.
- **Normalize breaks.** Tell her, "I've got the baby—go shower or nap."

You're not babysitting. You're parenting. She shouldn't need to ask. And just when you think you've seen it all, something else freaks you out. Spoiler: most of it's normal. Here's your decoder ring:

💬 **Reflection Prompt**
What's one thing I can do this week that she won't have to ask for—but will make her feel seen?

🧠 Dad Sanity Check
Am I helping or hovering? Fixing or supporting?

Here's a quick way to tell:

- Helping means doing without needing praise.
- Hovering means asking too many "Is this okay?" questions.
- Fixing means trying to make her feel better fast.
- Supporting means sitting with her, holding space—even if she's crying and you don't know why.

This is where your support matters most—not with speeches or grand gestures, but in the quiet, repeated acts that keep her standing. That's love in motion.

WTF Is This? (Totally Normal Edition)
Here's a quick hit list of stuff that might freak you out—but is actually normal in the first couple weeks.

What's Freaking You Out	Why It's (Probably) Normal
Lochia	Heavy post-birth bleeding. Looks intense but it's your partner's body clearing out.
Baby Acne	Little red bumps on the baby's face. Totally normal. Clears up on its own.
Cluster Feeding	Baby feeds constantly. Boosts supply—even though it feels endless. Snacks and water help.
Partner Crying Randomly	Overwhelmed, tired, hormonal—there might be tears. Just offer tissues and snacks.
Peeing During Laughing/ Sneezing	Her pelvic floor's recovering. Time (and possibly PT) will help.
Baby Poop Color Wheel	Black, green, mustard yellow—all normal. Gross, but expected.

Don't panic. Search smart: Mayo Clinic and AAP are solid. If something truly feels off, call the doc. Otherwise, deep breath—it's probably just new-parent normal.

Wrap-Up: You're In It Now—And That's a Good Thing
You've made it through the thick of the newborn phase. And yeah—it's messy, confusing, and downright exhausting. But you're still here. Still doing it. That counts for more than you probably realize.

No one's handing out trophies for perfect diaper changes—or who stayed up the longest. What matters is that you stayed in it. You didn't check out when it got hard. You didn't disappear when it got real.

You won't remember every burp or bottle. But you'll remember being there—wiping spit-up, reheating meals, keeping her company when she needed it most.

That's what being a good dad looks like. Not flawless—just present.

So if you're tired? Welcome to the club. If you're unsure? Join the rest of us. Just keep showing up. Your partner sees it. Your kid will grow up knowing it. There's nothing more dad than that.

PART 7

YOU, HER, AND THE LONG GAME OF TEAMWORK

*"One of the greatest things a father can do for his children is
to love their mother."*
—Howard W. Hunter

After our daughter was born, I figured the hard part was behind us. Turns out, that's when the real work started.

We were home, sleep-deprived, and trying to keep a newborn alive while my wife recovered from delivery—and I was figuring out how to be helpful without making things worse. It felt like we were both doing double shifts in the same house but barely crossing paths.

This phase isn't just diapers and sleep trades—it's relationship management on hard mode. You and your partner just went through something huge, and now you're healing in different ways under the same roof while raising a tiny human who gives zero thought to your bandwidth.

This part is about emotional intelligence—reading the room, checking your own temperature, and staying connected when you're both stretched thin.

Think of it like co-op mode in a tough game: you're not leading, not following—you're in it together. Talk like teammates, not managers. Protect each other's energy. Know when to offer help, step back, or admit you're tapped out.

Nobody teaches you this growing up—but it's some of the most important work you'll ever do. Not just for your partner, but for the kind of dad (and man) you're becoming.

You don't need to get everything right. You just need to stay connected—even when it's loud, messy, and neither of you knows what day it is.

This part is about keeping each other anchored. Next up: supporting recovery without burning out.

7.1: POSTPARTUM MENTAL HEALTH: HERS AND YOURS

Let's cut the bullshit—this isn't just hormones or "baby blues." You're both in a helluva mix: identity shifts, no sleep, major life reboots. She's healing from birth and maybe breastfeeding. You're juggling tasks, expectations, and exhaustion. That combo can rattle anyone.

Why It's More Than Hormones
It's not just her hormones tanking—it's your whole life flipped. No sleep, new roles, acting tough when you feel fragile. Pride. Fear. Overwhelm. You're both remaking your sense of self—and that's heavy.

Mental Health Red Flags for Both of You
Spot them like gear malfunctions—catching them early makes them easier to fix. Watch for:

- **Mood swings:** She's crying at dinner or snapping; you're foggy or irritable
- **Hopeless thoughts:** "I can't do this" (low but real)
- **Anxiety/panic:** Racing mind, chest tightness—not just tiredness
- **Withdrawal** from baby, partner, or life
- **Craving escape**—booze, screens, overwork—or feeling numb

Mental Health Red Flags for New Dads

You're not just support staff—you're in the blast zone too. These signs might sneak up on you, especially if you're trying to power through. Pay attention if you notice:

- Feeling disconnected or "not yourself"
- Eating or sleeping way more—or way less—than usual
- Constant guilt: "I'm failing her" or "I'm weak"
- Using habits to check out
- Worry about money or the future on a constant loop

So what does all that actually look like day-to-day? Here's your quick-view: what's normal stress, and what's a bigger flag waving at you.

What Postpartum Mental Health Struggles Can Look Like

It's not just her. Postpartum mental health challenges can hit both parents. Here's what to watch for—and where to go when you need backup.

For Her	For You
Persistent sadness, hopelessness, or guilt	Feeling numb or detached
Anxiety or panic attacks	Rage, irritability, or deep shame
Loss of interest in usual joys	Appetite, sleep, or energy changes
Trouble bonding with the baby	Escaping into work, gaming, alcohol, or isolation
Thoughts of self-harm or feeling like a "bad mom"	Feeling like you're failing or "not cut out for this"

Where to Get Help:

- Postpartum Support International: www.postpartum.net
- 988 Suicide & Crisis Lifeline: www.988lifeline.org

☑ **Quick Self-Check**

Even if you think you're fine, take 30 seconds to gut-check:

1. Am I sleeping—or just running on fumes and caffeine?
2. When's the last time I really laughed?
3. Do I feel connected to my partner—or just co-existing?
4. Have I told anyone what I'm actually feeling?
5. Am I escaping into screens, work, or booze more than usual?
6. What would I say if she were acting like I am?

Where to Start If You're Struggling

If the fog's getting thicker—or one of you seems off—don't wait it out. These are solid first moves when things feel heavy:

- **Call or text a friend or pro:** "Feeling low—can we talk?"
- **Use solid resources:**
  - Maternal Mental Health Hotline: 1-833-9-HELP4MOMS
  - Postpartum Support International: postpartum.net
- **Normalize therapy:** "We see doctors for colds—our brains need check-ins too."
- **Ask for help:** "Can you drop off dinner?" or "I need 20 minutes to breathe."

💡 **Dad Tip: Self-aware beats self-silent.**

The strongest dads aren't the quiet ones—they're the ones who name what's hard before it gets worse.

Your Role: Chief Sanity Officer

You're already handling a lot. This part's about protecting the mental load too—hers and yours. Not fixing, just showing up where it counts.

- Check in daily—not "How's the baby?" but "How are you feeling?"
- Listen without fixing—bad days, fears, aches. You don't have to solve them.
- Ask what she needs: sleep, food, quiet, laughs.
- Model honesty: "I'm wiped and shaky too." Breaking the silence matters.

Lifting her up means not sinking yourself. Keep both sides of the ship afloat.

Practical Moves You Both Can Use

These small moves can interrupt a spiral or defuse tension before it builds. Nothing fancy—just real actions that make the hard days more doable.

- Red Flag Triage: When her mood—or yours—goes sideways, try:
  - "This feels out of my wheelhouse. Can we chat?"
  - A sticky note that says "Grateful for you" where she'll see it.
- Quick mental reset: Even 5 minutes—breathing, walking, jotting stuff—can help more than you think.

♀ Dad Tips

Need a first step that's low effort but high impact?

- Online therapy is a legit lifeline (BetterHelp, Talkspace).
- You can even screen together: mentalhealthscreening.org.

⊕ Dad Sanity Check

What emotion am I hiding—pride, guilt, anger, fear? Write it. Say it. Own it. Still unsure if it's just exhaustion or something deeper? Try this 10-second gut check:

- Am I isolating?
- Do I feel resentful?
- Have I lost joy?

If these hit close, it's not weakness—it's your brain waving a flag. Don't ignore it.

♡ Reflection Prompt

What's one feeling I've been brushing off—and what's one small move I can take today to own it?

Save this page. Highlight, dog-ear, or screenshot it. These check-ins might be exactly what you need on a day everything feels upside-down.

You're not just surviving—you're building the resilience that holds your whole family up. This part is about keeping each other anchored. Next up: supporting recovery without burning out.

7.2: SURVIVAL TIP #7—TALK LIKE A TEAMMATE, NOT A MANAGER

A lot of new dads mean well—but end up sounding like they're running a warehouse shift. "You need to sleep." "You should take a break." "You have to eat something." The heart's in the right place, but the delivery misses.

The move: talk like a teammate, not a manager.

Saying "How can I help with…?" instead of "You need to…" shifts you from giving orders to actually collaborating. It tells your partner you're in this together—not just watching from the sidelines with a clipboard.

This is co-op parenting, not a solo run with a sidekick.
You're not leading the mission while she tags along. You're both in the game—sometimes one of us is carrying, sometimes you're both grinding. Either way, the win's shared.

💡 **Dad Tip: Weekly Huddle-Ups**
Once a week, pick a time to check in. Doesn't have to be deep or dramatic—10 minutes during a baby nap works. Sit, breathe, and run through a few simple questions.

🗣️ **Huddle-Up Questions**
- What's one thing that worked this week?
- What could we make easier next week?
- What's something we each need for ourselves?

This swaps silent resentment for shared strategy. You see what matters to her, and she hears what's real for you.

What Makes Communication Break Down—and How to Fix It

Even solid relationships get scrambled in newborn fog. You're both sleep-deprived, stressed, and probably communicating like two zombies passing in the night. Here are the pitfalls—and here's how to fix them.

Common Pitfalls:

- **Assuming instead of asking:** You guess she wants space, so you back off… but she actually needed help. Ask.
- **Resentment stacking:** You hold in every frustration until it blows over something dumb, like a burp cloth. Deal with the small stuff early.
- **Snapping without context:** You're not mad about the laundry. You're mad because you haven't slept and feel unseen. Say that instead.

Fixes That Actually Work:

- **Mirror what you hear:** "So you're saying you feel like everything's on your shoulders right now?" Simple but powerful.
- **Use "we" more than "you":** "We've both been stretched thin—how do we rebalance this?"
- **Be specific when asking for help:** "Can you hold the baby while I shower?" beats "I need a break."
- **Hit reset if things go sideways:** "Can we pause and start over? I want to do this right." It's a circuit breaker, not a cop-out—and it's saved me more times than I can count.

Communication Cheat Sheet

If you only remember three things when you're running on fumes, make it these. Pin it to the fridge, save it in your phone—just don't forget it.

- Listen to understand—not to win
- Ask instead of assuming
- When in doubt, hug

Print it. Post it. Live it.

💡 **Dad Tip**

Use a shared calendar, whiteboard, or notes app. Even a fridge list helps turn chaos into clarity. We treat our calendar app like a second brain—keeps things from falling through the cracks.

🐢 **Dad Sanity Check**

Am I offering help—or assuming I know what she needs? When's the last time I really asked?

💬 **Reflection Prompt**

When's the last time I asked what she really needs—instead of guessing? And what's one small shift I can make this week to talk like her teammate, not her manager?

7.3: HANDLING STRESS, OPINIONS, AND FEELING OUT OF YOUR DEPTH

You're about to get flooded with input—and most of it won't help. Family, friends, coworkers—everyone's got "expert" parenting advice. Some's gold. A lot isn't.

Call it what it is—well-meaning noise. Your job? Sort the useful from the useless and guard your family's flow.

Why It Hits Different for Dads
You're wired to fix things. But raising a baby isn't a home project—it's messy, slow, and constantly changing. That mismatch wears you down fast.

Here's the thing: Setting boundaries isn't rude—it's survival. If someone's input feels like pressure, you can thank them and move on. Try:

- "We appreciate your experience—we'll keep it in mind."
- "That's not the route we're going, but thanks."
- "Let me check with [partner] and get back to you."

No debate—just hold the line.

⊙ **Family Opinions Survival Guide**

Getting steamrolled with family advice? Here's your mini armor kit:

- Smile, nod, don't explain
- "We're figuring out what works for us"
- "Thanks, we'll keep that in mind."

Use on repeat. You don't owe anyone a play-by-play of your parenting choices.

When Overwhelm Kicks In

You're doing something huge—keeping a tiny human alive while learning everything on the fly. Overwhelm is part of the gig.

Here's how to keep from spiraling:

- **Write it down.** Get the stress out of your head and into your notes app. Instant relief.
- **Talk it out.** Partner, friend, fellow dad—pick someone who listens more than they lecture.
- **Ask, don't assume.** "Would it help if I...?" is way better than guessing and missing.

💡 **Dad Tip: You don't need all the answers—just keep showing up.**
Consistency beats expertise. Even when you're not sure what to do, your presence says, "I'm in this."

🗣 Boundary Scripts for Dads

- "Thanks—that sounds helpful. We'll think it over."
- "We're doing something different, but we appreciate the thought."
- "I'll check with [partner] and let you know."
- "That works for some people—just not our style."

Short. Polite. Done.

Unsolicited Opinions and the Mental Load

Someone will always chime in—especially when the baby's crying, your partner's healing, or you're running on fumes. It piles onto your already maxed-out brain.

Here's your move—filter, don't absorb.

Mentally tag advice into three simple buckets:

- Helpful: "We'll try that."
- Maybe later: "Not for us right now."
- Hard pass: "Thanks, but nope."

Labeling it helps you stay in control.

💡 Dad Tip: Curate Your Feed

If parenting content on social makes you feel behind—unfollow, mute, or log out. Confidence is built in real life, not comparison reels.

🎙 Real Talk

When my wife's dad came to stay with us for a few months after the baby was born, I wasn't sure what to think. The man's a seasoned pro—four kids, with my wife as the first. He meant well and genuinely helped out… but it got tricky. At first, I kept my head down and tried to roll with it. But every diaper change felt like I was being judged by a parenting referee. If I held the baby "wrong" or didn't bounce her the "right" way, there was always a comment. I started second-guessing myself.

Eventually, I brought it up with my wife. She heard me out and said, "Maybe it's time we ask him for a little space, but let him know we're thankful." She had the first conversation with him, and then we all talked together. We made it clear we appreciated everything he'd done, but we needed to find our own rhythm—even if it looked messy.

It wasn't easy, but it brought peace back into the house. It gave us room to figure things out as a team—and gave me space to be the dad I was becoming, not a rerun of someone else's playbook.

Feeling Out of Your Depth

You'll have moments where you feel like you're screwing it all up. That's normal. Here's how to reset:

- **Ask for clarity:** "What's the most helpful thing I can do right now?"
- **Douse one flame:** Diaper. Bottle. Dishes. Small wins count.
- **Don't isolate—reach out.** Text a dad friend. Say, "This is a lot."

You're not alone, even if it feels like it.

When Stress Boils Over

Not every meltdown moment needs a full reset. Sometimes you just need a quick release valve—step outside, crack a joke in your notes app, or just say out loud, "This is a lot." Tiny moves bleed off pressure before it builds.

Dad Reset Toolkit

Need a mid-chaos reboot? Keep this in your back pocket:

1. Step outside for 2 minutes
2. Do 10 slow breaths
3. Text your buddy "WTF" and regroup

Tiny moves. Big difference.

♀ **Dad Tip: Anger vs. Burnout—Know the Signs Before You Snap**

Not all outbursts are about anger—sometimes it's just pure exhaustion. Here's how to catch it early:

- You're more irritable than usual, even over small stuff
- You start avoiding the baby or your partner
- You feel numb or checked out, not just frustrated
- You can't focus or make simple decisions

If this sounds like you, hit pause. Step away. Tag in your partner or support system. Burnout isn't weakness—it's a warning.

🧠 Dad Sanity Check
- What pressure am I carrying that I didn't ask for?
- Is this stress based on what's expected—or what's actually needed?
- Who can I talk to today just to get this off my chest?

💬 Reflection Prompt
What's one piece of advice or pressure I've been carrying that doesn't actually fit us—and how can I let it go this week?

🎙 Real Talk: What I Wish I Knew About My Own Mental Health
I wasn't ready when we found out we were pregnant. And I definitely felt a kind of loss—loss of my old life, loss of all the 'what could've been' stuff like late-night movies and stress-free weekends. No one really talks about that part. I wish I'd known it's okay to grieve the life you're leaving behind and still love the one you're stepping into. More advice isn't always help. This job is messy, unpredictable, and deeply personal. The best move? Keep showing up. Trust your instincts. Protect your peace. It's enough.

7.4: SEX, CLOSENESS, AND PLANNING THE NEXT CHAPTER

After the baby's born, everything shifts—including how you think about sex, connection, and what's next. One moment you're in survival mode. The next, you're wondering when—or if—you'll feel close again. The truth? It's about more than sex—it's safety, timing, trust, and starting slow, without guilt or pressure.

This part of the relationship gets weird—and that's okay. What matters most now is mutual respect, patience, and clear communication.

Physical Recovery Plus Emotional Readiness Equals A Moving Target

Doctors throw out "six weeks" like it's a magic number—but healing and readiness don't follow a clock. Here's why the timeline is more complex:

1. Six weeks isn't magic. It's a guideline, not a green light. Her body might be physically healed, but emotionally she might still feel miles away from wanting anything close to sex. That's not rejection—it's reality.

2. Breastfeeding affects hormones. Lower estrogen means lower libido and vaginal dryness. That's just biology. Grab the lube. Keep it gentle. Always ask first.

3. C-section or tearing? Add recovery time, soreness, and sometimes nerve sensitivity. Always check in first.

What's Normal vs. Red Flags

Healing isn't one-size-fits-all. Here's the quick gut check:

- **Normal:** Some soreness, dryness (especially with breastfeeding), or just feeling nervous about being close again.
- **Red flags:** Sharp pain, bleeding, fever, or pulling away emotionally and never bouncing back.

If you're unsure, don't guess—suggest calling her OB. And instead of asking, "So... sex?" **try:** "How are you feeling about being close again—no pressure, just curious where your head's at?"

When One of You Wants It—and the Other Doesn't

Here's the hard part: sometimes, your drive doesn't match hers. Maybe you're craving that connection. Maybe she's nowhere near that headspace. That mismatch is common—but left unspoken, it turns into resentment fast.

Your job is to not make her feel broken, guilty, or like she's disappointing you.

Her job isn't to ignore how you're feeling.

This is where communication matters most. Say, "I miss us—but I also want to respect where you are. How can we stay close in ways that feel good for both of us?"

Breastfeeding Does Not Equal Birth Control

Let me say this louder: **breastfeeding is not birth control.**

🎙 **Real Talk**

My wife got pregnant again when our daughter was just 6 months old… her body wasn't ready, and we lost that pregnancy at 13 weeks. It broke us.

We never want another dad to go through that blindly.

Talk about contraception now—not after. Options include:

- Condoms: Easy, instant, no hormones.
- IUDs: Low maintenance, long-term, very effective.
- The mini-pill: Breastfeeding-safe. Needs daily use.
- Implants or shots: Long-lasting, hormone-based.

Talk to her OB. Make the appointment together if needed. Birth control is your responsibility too.

What Intimacy Looks Like Now

If sex is off the table, closeness is still on it. Right now, intimacy is about small, low-pressure moves that remind her she's more than "mom" and you're more than "roommates."

It looks like:

- Sitting shoulder-to-shoulder on the couch, even if you're both half-dead tired
- Holding her hand during a 3 a.m. feeding so she doesn't feel alone
- Saying "I love you" or "I miss you" with zero agenda
- Laughing together about something dumb—like the baby fart that scared the dog
- A forehead kiss, a hand on her back, or a shoulder rub with no strings attached
- Sending a quick "you good?" text in the middle of the day—something kind, not just logistics
- Sitting together with no phones, even for five quiet minutes

- Making real eye contact—not the creepy stare, but the "I actually see you" kind
- Telling her she's still sexy—without expecting anything back
- Asking: "What helps you feel close right now?" ... then actually listening

These aren't throwaway moves. They're the glue that keeps you connected when everything else feels like chaos.

Ways to Reconnect Without Pressure

When you're both running on fumes, keep it simple. These land every time:

- Shoulder rub, no strings
- Quick walk around the block
- Five quiet minutes, no phones
- A "you good?" text that's not about diapers
- "I love you" or "I miss you"—with zero agenda

♀ Dad Tip: Intimacy Does Not Equal Sex

Connection doesn't start in the bedroom—it starts with how you show up during the day. Warm words, small gestures, and zero expectations go farther than you think. Physical closeness will come. Safety and trust have to get there first.

Planning the Next Baby—Or Not

Even if baby #2 isn't on your mind yet, it's worth talking timelines. According to the WHO and ACOG, it's best to wait at least 18 months between pregnancies. That spacing gives her body time to fully recover and reduces risks of miscarriage, premature birth, and complications.

Have the conversation early:

- "Are we okay with this timeline?"
- "What would we need to feel ready again?"
- "What's the plan if we're not ready but get a surprise?"

Dad Sanity Check
- Have I assumed she's "fine now" because it's been a few weeks?
- Have I checked in without pressuring—or just backed off entirely?
- Am I avoiding the birth control talk because it's awkward or scary?

You don't need all the answers. What matters is openness, patience, and the guts to talk about hard stuff—even when it's awkward.

Reflection Prompt
What's one small way I can help my partner feel cared for—without expecting anything in return?

Wrap-Up: You're Not Just a Parent—You're a Partner
By now, you know there's no script for this. No checklist that guarantees closeness or calm. But you *can* control how you show up, how you listen, and how you treat the person raising this tiny human alongside you.

More small kindnesses, fewer assumptions. More "How can I help?" and less "You should…" That's how you keep the team vibe alive—even when the wheels feel like they're coming off.

You're building trust, resilience, and emotional muscle that'll carry into every season of parenting. Stay honest. Stay connected. Stay human.

You're not just getting through this—you're learning how to lead from beside. That's what real fatherhood looks like.

FURTHER READING AND RESOURCES FOR FIRST-TIME DADS

If you've made it this far, you're either still hungry for more—or you're scrolling the internet one-handed while holding a baby. Either way, here's your dad-approved reference list. Every source here shaped the tips in this book and is backed by science, real-life usefulness, or both.

PREGNANCY, BIRTH, AND BABY CARE

American Academy of Pediatrics (AAP)

Trusted guidance on newborn care, vaccines, safe sleep, and baby milestones.

- American Academy of Pediatrics. (n.d.). HealthyChildren.org. Retrieved March 2025, from https://www.healthychildren.org

Centers for Disease Control and Prevention (CDC)

Evidence-based info on pregnancy health, child development, and immunizations.

- Centers for Disease Control and Prevention. (n.d.). Pregnancy and child development. Retrieved March 2025, from https://www.cdc.gov

Mayo Clinic

Clear, reliable breakdowns of symptoms, pregnancy stages, and baby care basics.

- Mayo Clinic. (2023). Pregnancy, birth, and newborn care. Retrieved March 2025, from https://www.mayoclinic.org

American College of Obstetricians and Gynecologists (ACOG)

Your go-to for what's medically normal, what to ask the OB, and how to prep for birth.

- American College of Obstetricians and Gynecologists. (n.d.). Pregnancy FAQs and guidelines. Retrieved March 2025, from https://www.acog.org

La Leche League International (LLLI)
Support for feeding—breastfeeding, pumping, or troubleshooting cluster feeds.

- La Leche League International. (n.d.). Breastfeeding and parenting resources. Retrieved March 2025, from https://www.llli.org

Sleep Foundation
Science-backed advice on newborn sleep, safe routines, and managing your own exhaustion.

- Sleep Foundation. (n.d.). Infant sleep and safety. Retrieved March 2025, from https://www.sleepfoundation.org

MENTAL HEALTH AND POSTPARTUM SUPPORT
Postpartum Support International (PSI)
A must-have for understanding postpartum depression, anxiety, and how to support your partner (and yourself).

- Postpartum Support International. (n.d.). Mental health resources for parents. Retrieved March 2025, from https://www.postpartum.net

National Institute of Mental Health (NIMH)
Clear breakdowns of postpartum symptoms and when to seek help.

- National Institute of Mental Health. (n.d.). Postpartum depression facts. Retrieved March 2025, from https://www.nimh.nih.gov

World Health Organization (WHO)
Postpartum care guidelines from a global perspective—mental, emotional, and physical.

- World Health Organization. (2018). Postpartum care guidelines. Retrieved March 2025, from https://www.who.int

BOOKS THAT DON'T SUCK

Simkin, P. (2018). The Birth Partner (5th ed.). Harvard Common Press.
A real-deal guide for being useful in the delivery room—catching the baby or just holding the leg.

Greenberg, G. & Hayden, J. (2004). Be Prepared: A Practical Handbook for New Dads. Simon & Schuster.
Funny, practical, and actually helpful—think survival manual with diapers.

Brott, A. (2021). The Expectant Father (5th ed.). Abbeville Press.
A classic go-to for expectant dads who want the full month-by-month breakdown.

Oster, E. (2019). Cribsheet: A Data-Driven Guide to Better, More Relaxed Parenting. Penguin Press.
If you like numbers and no-BS analysis, this book breaks down baby decisions using data, not drama.

Gottman, J. & Gottman, J. (2017). And Baby Makes Three. Harmony Books.
Science-backed ways to keep your relationship strong once the baby lands.

DAD-FRIENDLY APPS, COMMUNITIES, AND TOOLS

DaddyUp
Pregnancy tracking designed for dads—part wilderness guide, part comic relief.

- DaddyUp. (n.d.). The dad's field guide to pregnancy. Retrieved March 2025, from https://www.daddyup.com

The Wonder Weeks
Helps decode your baby's mental leaps (and mood swings) during the first 20 months.

- The Wonder Weeks. (n.d.). Baby development app. Retrieved March 2025, from https://www.thewonderweeks.com

Reddit – r/daddit & r/predaddit

Real-life stories, humor, and support from dads who've been through it—or are still in the thick of it.

- Reddit. (n.d.). Dad communities. Retrieved March 2025, from https://www.reddit.com

That's your quick-access toolkit. Now, let's zoom out for a second... because resources are great, but they're nothing without you in the mix.

CONCLUSION:
YOU'RE IN IT—AND YOU'RE DOING IT

Hey man,

Pause. Breathe. Let this sink in—you didn't just finish the book, you pushed through one of the biggest reboots of your life.

You didn't just read about pregnancy, birth, and newborn chaos—you showed up. You pushed through the hard parts, the awkward parts, the "what the hell am I doing?" moments. And that matters way more than perfect nursery lighting or a flawless day-one swaddle.

The whole time, you've been doing something most dads never get—a real-deal user guide, written for you, with you in mind.

Because this was never about getting it all right. It's about being present, consistent, and in the game.

Looking Ahead
So… now what?

You keep showing up—one bottle, one late-night diaper, one "we've got this" at a time.

You'll second-guess yourself. You'll get frustrated. You'll have weird moments when you miss silence, clean clothes, or your old kind of free time.

But then—just like that—your baby locks eyes with you, flashes that gummy smile, or crashes asleep on your chest… and suddenly, everything rewrites itself.

You don't need to be the perfect dad. You just need to be your baby's dad: present, human, learning out loud.

💡 Final Dad Tip: Keep Showing Up

You won't always feel like you know what you're doing. You'll mess up burps, freeze when the baby screams, or say the wrong thing at the wrong time. Welcome to the club.

But the thing that changes everything? You—showing up.

Tired. Clueless. Still trying.

That's what your partner and your baby will remember. That's what builds trust. That's what makes a dad.

If This Book Helped You...

Thanks for letting me be in your corner—and for trusting me to walk with you through the mess and the magic.

If this book made you feel seen, prepared, or a little more confident, here are **two quick things** that make a huge difference for small, independent authors like me:

- **Leave a review.** It only takes a minute, but it matters more than you think. Reviews help other dads find this book—and they keep independent voices like mine alive. Drop one wherever you bought it.
- **Pass it on.** Got a friend staring at a pregnancy test? A coworker heading to the delivery room? A buddy deep in newborn mode and second-guessing everything? Share this book with him—he might need to hear the same words you did.

Then tell him what I'm telling you right now:

You are enough.

You've got what you need—and who you need.

Now go be the dad only you can be.

You're a dad now—and that's the point.

—Cameron (a dad like you)

ACKNOWLEDGMENTS

This book wouldn't exist without the people who kept me sane, caffeinated, and brutally honest through the chaos of new fatherhood.

First, to my wife, **Rhowela**—you didn't just make me a dad, you made me better. Thank you for believing in this project, for your edits and eye rolls, and for loving me through every awkward metaphor and midnight writing sprint.

To **Emerie** and **Averie**, my girls—my giggle factories and my daily reminders that love is loud, messy, and worth every second. You made me a dad, and you make me want to keep showing up.

To my **brothers and close friends**—thank you for answering late-night texts, offering real talk, and reminding me I wasn't in this alone. You're part of this story, whether you meant to be or not.

And **to the dad reading this**—thanks for caring enough to be here. You're already doing better than you probably think.

MORE SUPPORT IF YOU WANT

You've just made it through one of the biggest reboots of your life, and you're still standing. Let's keep that momentum rolling.

I've flagged these along the way, but I pulled them together here so you've got everything in one place.

Dad Survival Toolkit

- **Early Dad Game Plan** – The starter pack for what you actually need (and nothing you don't).
- **Dad Leave Cheat Sheet** – Maximize your time off without losing your mind or your paycheck.
- **Birth Plan Snapshot** – A quick, clear version you can actually follow in the heat of the moment.
- **Hospital Bag Checklist for Dads** – What to pack so you're useful, comfortable, and not panic-buying snacks at the gift shop at 2 a.m.
- **Month-by-Month Dad Survival Guide** – What's coming, what's normal, and how to stay steady through it.

Grab them here:
subscribepage.io/juniperdylan-bonuses

or through this QR code.

For Your Partner
If your partner wants the same kind of real talk, my wife's built some seriously helpful resources at **rhowelaafriel.com**.

You've got this, man. And now you've got a few more tools in your corner.

ABOUT THE AUTHOR

Cameron is a husband, girl dad, and proud Michigander who knows what it's like to feel unprepared and figure things out the hard way. He served as a Navy Corpsman with the Marines, where he learned about friendship, purpose, and showing up for your team—lessons that shaped the way he approaches fatherhood today.

After the Navy, Cameron went back to school while working long hours— sometimes biking or catching the bus just to get there. Like most dads, he's juggled late nights, early mornings, and plenty of "what am I doing?" moments. Those struggles taught him the same principles he writes about here: show up, listen first, and find the humor in the chaos.

These days, Cameron's happiest chasing his two daughters, Emerie and Averie, around the backyard with his wife, Rhowela, nearby—usually with s'mores or a campfire involved.

He wrote "You're a Dad Now" for regular guys who want to be present, intentional, and human through one of the biggest changes of their lives.

www.ingramcontent.com/pod-product-compliance
Lightning Source LLC
LaVergne TN
LVHW052027080426
835513LV00018B/2211